The
COLLECTED POEMS
of FAY ZWICKY

ABOUT THE AUTHOR

Fay Zwicky has published eight books of poetry, the most recent of which is *Picnic* (Giramondo, 2006). She has also edited several anthologies of Australian poetry, published a book of short stories, *Hostages* (FACP, 1983), and a collection of critical essays, *The Lyre in the Pawnshop* (UWAP, 1986). Her awards include the NSW Premier's Literary Award, the Western Australian Premier's Book Award, the Patrick White Literary Award and the FAW Christopher Brennan Award, celebrating lifetime achievement in poetry.

The COLLECTED POEMS of FAY ZWICKY

Edited & introduced by
LUCY DOUGAN &
TIM DOLIN

UWA PUBLISHING

First published in 2017 by
UWA Publishing
Crawley, Western Australia 6009
www.uwap.uwa.edu.au

UWAP is an imprint of UWA Publishing
a division of The University of Western Australia

This book is copyright. Apart from any fair dealing for the purpose of private study, research, criticism or review, as permitted under the *Copyright Act 1968*, no part may be reproduced by any process without written permission. Enquiries should be made to the publisher.

Copyright © Fay Zwicky 2017
The moral right of the author has been asserted.

National Library of Australia
Cataloguing-in-Publication data:
Zwicky, Fay, 1933– author.
The collected poems of Fay Zwicky / Fay Zwicky;
Lucy Dougan, Tim Dolin, editors
ISBN: 9781742589329 (paperback)
Includes bibliographical references.
Australian poetry—21st century.
Other Creators/Contributors:
Dougan, Lucy, editor.
Dolin, Tim, editor.

Cover photograph by Jacqueline Mitelman
Typeset in Bembo by Lasertype
Printed by Lightning Source

This project has been assisted by the Australian Government through the Australia Council, its arts funding and advisory body.

 uwapublishing

With thanks to all those
who brought this book to life

Contents

Introduction by Lucy Dougan and Tim Dolin — 1
Note on the Text — 11
Acknowledgements — 12
Border Crossings (2000) — 13

ISAAC BABEL'S FIDDLE

Perspective — 29
Survival Kit — 30
An Australian — 31
To a Sea Horse — 32
Isaac Babel's Fiddle Reaches the Indian Ocean — 33
In Memory of Ries Mulder — 37
For Anna — 38
Orpheus — 39
The Name of the Game — 40
Respite — 41
The Gift — 43
Emily Dickinson Judges the Bread Division
    at the Amherst Cattle Show, 1858 — 44
Lear, Class '71 — 47
Catullus at Sirmio — 49
Spinoza's Lens — 50
Summer Pogrom — 51
Song of Experience — 52
And Innocence? — 53
Gall Tripartite — 54
Totem and Taboo — 56
The Chosen—Kalgoorlie, 1894 — 58
Forbearance—Coolgardie, 1898 — 60
Don Juan at the Record Bar — 61
Chicken — 62
Scoop — 64
A Midwestern Wife — 65
Memorial Day & Tornado — 68
4-Lane Divided — 70

vii

Fungus Epidemic	71
The Garden of the F'u Dogs	72
Little League	73
Dogwood	74
Leaving Chicago in December	75
Republican Attorney & Client	76
Waking	77
The Prodigy Ages	78
Lot's Wife (Take 18)	79
Projection Box	80
Paperbacks	81
Maharishi Consolator	83
Charity Ball	85
Campus Fable	86
Tea Room	87
Literary Board	88

KADDISH

Kaddish	91
Cleft	98
Dreams	99
The Artist	100
Identity	102
After Such Knowledge	103
Reckoning	104
Three Songs of Love & Hate	105
1. The Stone Dolphin	105
2. Jack Frost	107
3. Tiger Heart	108
Lamb	109
Ark Voices	110
Mrs Noah Speaks	110
Lemur	114
Bat	116
Mouse	118
Mink	119
Wolf-Song	121
Tiger	124

Hippo Sonnets		126
Giraffe		127
Whale Psalm		129
Elephant		131
The Poet Gives a Reading		132
The Poet Puts It Away		135
The Poet Asks Forgiveness		138

ASK ME

I

China Poems 1988		141
I	Roosters and Earthworms	141
II	Out of This World	143
III	Over the Wall	146
IV	Passing	148
Tiananmen Square June 4, 1989		149
The Temple, Somnapura		151
I	Ganesh	151
II	Vishnu	155
III	Siva	158
IV	Devi	161
Four Poems from America		165
I	Father in a Mirror	165
II	Southern Spell	166
III	Jack Frost in Florida	167
IV	Band Music for a Grandfather	168
A Tale of the Great Smokies		169
1	Otis Makes a Wheel	169
2	Penelope Spins	171
3	Uriah Mack behind the Sassafras	173
4	Otis Raises Sheep	175
5	Penelope and the Lambs	178
6	Uriah is Hired by Otis	181
7	The Shearing	183
8	The Dyeing	185

II

Broadway Vision	187
The Call	191

Pie in the Sky	193
For A.D. Hope	197
Growing Up	199
Reading a Letter in Amsterdam	200
The Ballad of the Pretty Young Wife	202
Jacques Tati at the Darwin Hotel	205
Marius in Hobart, 1989	207
New Age	210
Miss Short Instructs Her Latin Class on the Fountains of Nepenthe, 1912	211

III

Hospice Training	215
Breathing Exercises	217
Afloat	218
Call It Love	219
Reading	220
Home Care	222
Soup and Jelly	226
In Memory, Vincent Buckley	228
For Jim	231

THE GATEKEEPER'S WIFE

The Gatekeeper's Wife	239
Orpheus	244
Losing Track	245
Poems and Things	247
Campaign Instructions	249
What Fills	251
Banksia blechifolia	252
Triple Exposure & Epilogue	253
The Caller	253
Bride Drinking from a Pool	255
Portrait	257
Epilogue: Wiping the Canvas	260
Finding Focus	262
Learning	263
Café Sitters	266
Letter from Claudia in the Midi	267

On the Acquisition of Four Famous Chinese Novels for the Senior Library & Related Matters	271
Shelley Plain	273
Groundswell for Ginsberg	274
Peminangan	278
Perdjodohan	279
Kera Kera	281
Akibat	283
Conference Hi-Jinks	284
A Summation	284
American Safety Valve	286
A Laureate Comes to Lunch	289
A Canterbury Tale	292
I.M. William Hart-Smith	293

PICNIC

Picnic	297
Close-up	300
Hokusai on the Shore	302
Aceh, December 2004	303
The Young Men	304
Makassar, 1956	305
Deckchair on the Titanic	310
External Affairs, 2nd Century AD	311
The Terracotta Army at Xi'an	313
1 The Emperor Qinshihuang	313
2 The Spear Bearer	315
3 The Cook	316
4 The Farrier	318
5 The Archer	320
6 The Potter	322
Coming and Going	325
Isfahan	327
Rhyme for a Granddaughter	328
Guy Fawkes Night, 2002	329
Letting Go	331
The Duck-Herd's Night Off	333
Push or Knock	334

Talking Mermaid	337
The Age of Aquarius	340
No Return	342
Interrogation	343
The Ivy Visitant	344
World Cup Spell 1998	347
Starting Over in Autumn	349
Adios, Buenos Aires	351
Cogito	352
Genesis	355
Poetry Promenaded	357

NEW AND UNCOLLECTED POEMS

Bedfellows	361
Madam C	363
Domestic Architecture	364
A Small Variant on Intelligence	366
Primal Dreamcake	367
Banksia Menziesii	370
Casting the Die	371
The Witnesses	374
Pages	375
My Dachshund Schnitzel	377
Reasons for Play	378
Charon	380
Little Fly	382
In Rehab	383
Boat Song	385
Droughtbreaker	386
In Memoriam, JB	387

Introduction

Lucy Dougan and Tim Dolin

Gathered here for the first time are Fay Zwicky's seven collections of poetry, published between 1975 and 2006, along with previously uncollected poems Zwicky has chosen to preserve, and her essay 'Border Crossings' (hereafter 'BC'), which eloquently and engagingly records the growth of her imagination and provides valuable insights into the atmosphere and character of her formative years. Zwicky has had a long and distinguished career in the arts: first as a classical pianist; later as a literature teacher, literary critic, editor, and sometime short-story writer; but foremost as a poet. She has not been in the public eye very much in recent years—like many of her generation she has chosen not to go online—but nor has she remained silent. She has written and published individual poems and maintained the journal that she has been keeping almost continuously for more than forty years. A writer's commonplace book, a poetry workbook, and a record of Zwicky's responses to private and public events, the journal integrates an impassioned dialogue with what she is reading, often satirical accounts of her dreams, and candid (as well as guarded) quarrels with herself, friends and family, ideas, opinions, and the whole business of living a literary and creative life. One of the journal's big recurring questions, indeed, is: how does a poet sustain a creative life at all in the unpromising soil of an isolated city on the edge of a desert? How does she go on fighting, in James Tulip's words, 'to affirm over and against an oppressive Australian silence a human (and particularly a woman's) voice and feeling' (31–32)?

Zwicky's humanism is the product of a mind and imaginative temperament shaped in a secular upper-middle-class Jewish household in postwar Melbourne, where European high culture was immensely valued, and educated Australians still felt themselves to be exiled from what A. D. Hope sardonically called 'civilisation over there.' Her formal literary education began at the Melbourne Church of England Girls' Grammar School (Merton Hall), and continued at the University of Melbourne, where, against all departmental advice, she undertook a thesis entitled 'The problem of evil: freedom, suffering and self-assertion in the novels of Dostoevsky.' This experience left its mark on her intellectual development and informed her sense of literature's moral seriousness, particularly when the young Sam Goldberg, who had returned from Cambridge to Melbourne, began the lectures that would in time transform academic literary studies there and elsewhere in Australia. But Zwicky's artistic and critical interests would soon take her to

America, and much of her art and thought have been the product of an Australian poet's dialogue with American individualism, internationalism, modernism, and the urbane intellectual humanism that was summed up in Lionel Trilling's phrase 'the liberal imagination.' Zwicky's earlier poetry is distinguished by its sincerity, its consciousness of the 'power of tradition' (Indyk, 'Moralist' 33), its conviction of the artist's responsibility, and its modernist struggle to assert an individual poetic voice in conditions inimical to the making of poetry. In the volumes published after 1990, Zwicky's poetry becomes more overtly political even as it becomes more personal and colloquial, as if a freeing up of poetic form contributes to the liberal work of creating a space for openness and dialogue. As Lisa Gorton has shown, Zwicky relinquishes the brilliance of the earlier mode for, in Zwicky's own words, 'the grace of candour' ('Starting Over in Autumn')—and, we might add, humility, and the empathy that can be expressed through dramatic forms and the interplay of different voices and modes.

As Zwicky herself has remarked, 'a writer has to emerge from family, religion and other ties' (Schwartz 9). She was born Julia Rosefield (Fay is her middle name) on 4 July 1933, and raised in the Melbourne bayside suburb of Brighton, the eldest of three sisters. As children they became the Rosefield Trio, a violinist, cellist, and pianist who toured Australia between 1946 and 1950 and were broadcast on ABC's 'Young Australia' and adult education programs. Zwicky's mother was a musician, and the driving force in their lives; her father, whose family were Lithuanian and German, was a medical doctor who spent six years at the war in Europe and died when he was away at sea in 1967. These early years she recalls as being 'Brontëan': meaning, perhaps, that what remains with her most is the intensity of an almost exclusively female life in 'a home of some turbulence' ('BC'). They were rambunctious, talented children in a household, and a cultural milieu, in which respectability, expectations, standards and a 'cranky moral earnestness' ('BC') were highly valued. And yet it was also a culturally liberal upbringing, albeit in a fashion-conscious haute-bourgeois way (Zwicky's mother decorated the house with the once voguish reproduction of a death mask known as 'L'Inconnue de la Seine' and served toheroa soup at dinner parties). The girls' imaginative lives and intellectual and material ambitions were taken seriously and they were offered rich artistic and educational opportunities. When books were asked for, they appeared. When *Bleak House* was serialised on the radio, Zwicky stayed home from school to listen to it in full. From the very beginning, words and music vied for her attention. There was always 'the book inside the music that I was supposed to be practising and my fingers were doing the work but my mind was reading the book' (Schwartz 9).

At the end of her degree Zwicky did a stint at the *Meanjin* desk with Clem Christesen, whose 'journal of ideas,' already a vital part of Australian letters, was 'built around books, to encourage free expression and intelligent criticism, to put forward "advance guard" material, [and] develop contacts abroad' (AustLit). The magazine's aim of situating Australian literature and ideas in the wider world was of a piece with other cultural enterprises in Australia at that time and made an impression on Zwicky. It was here, too, that she dealt firsthand with new work by many established figures in Australian writing. When she arrived in the early 1950s, Christesen had been publishing Judith Wright for many years, and the *Meanjin* circle at that time also included R. D. FitzGerald, Vance and Nettie Palmer, Xavier Herbert, Katharine Susannah Prichard, and Manning Clark. Christesen was to publish many of Zwicky's important early poems in the 1970s.

After completing her musical studies, Zwicky worked as a touring concert pianist for the Dutch Bond van Kunstkringen and the British Council in Indonesia, Singapore and Malaya from the mid-fifties, and then as a lecturer in English in Bandung, West Java, where she met her husband, the Swiss biologist Karl Zwicky. After a period in Europe they settled in Perth where they raised two children, and where Zwicky worked for 26 years in the Department of English at The University of Western Australia as a specialist in American literature, first as a senior tutor, then from 1972 as a senior lecturer. Perth is one of the most remote capital cities in the world, and for new arrivals in 1961 it must have seemed very isolated. Yet just as her work as a musician had afforded her opportunities to travel, so too did her poetry. Zwicky has visited and had residencies in the USA, UK, China, and elsewhere, and over the years formed close associations with leading poets such as Charles Causley, Helen Adam, Mark Strand, Robert Creeley, Robert Duncan, John Unterecker, Judith Hemschemeyer, and Mark Rudman.

Zwicky was first in the USA in 1965–66 doing a postgraduate study of Bach's 48 Preludes and Fugues for performance on the harpsichord with Edward Kilenyi, successor to Ernst von Dohnányi at the Florida State University in Tallahassee. Most of the year 1972–73 was spent establishing a creative writing unit for mature-age students at the University of Illinois in Urbana. She finally found the ideal conditions for the emergence of her own poetic voice in 1978–79 when she was Visiting Scholar in Columbia University's creative writing program on the recommendation of Robert Creeley. On that occasion she gave public readings at the legendary Chumley's in the city, and 'Kaddish,' probably her best known and most admired poem, was first published in Columbia's literary magazine *Antaeus*. While in New York she also worked with William Weaver on an issue of the journal *Translations*. Her knowledge of American literature and culture is deep, and although she found much in the New York literary scene congenial, she also sometimes felt alien there. More broadly, too, her time in America made her understand the value of her Australianness and at the same time inspired a deep sense of kinship with, and home feeling in, the USA. Indeed, to Schwartz she confessed that 'at times, she wished she'd been born in America rather than pre-war Australia, "so that I would be not ashamed of what seemed like my foreign interloper status"' (9).

Zwicky felt such a strong sense of belonging in America, ironically, because of that country's rich tradition of writers and artists imaginatively liberated by their foreign background. Exile can be a luxury, she remarks in 'Border Crossings,' and being an outsider is a rich heritage shared by her touchstone poets Donne, Blake, Shelley, Hopkins, Dickinson, Whitman, Lawrence, and Ginsberg. Australia, like America, was 'a country where you can re-invent yourself over and over again' ('BC'). But her 'dissenting imagination' ('BC') shunned the solitariness of the Australian poetic condition and craved the communities of outsiders that flourished in Ginsberg's America. There she discovered that being Jewish, being 'a stranger both to one's own and to one's adopted culture' ('BC'), freed her up to reconfigure and refresh language and ideas from widely divergent cultural traditions. In America, too, poetic culture and practice were attuned historically to the eloquence, vitality and poetic potential of American common speech, with its self-confidence and democratic optimism, and some of her best and most interesting poems are in the mode of Americana. The sharp contrast with Australian conditions, despite the similarities she saw between the two physical and cultural environments, was an ongoing preoccupation for Zwicky (most importantly, they share only a 'superficial concept of democracy,' she observed [*Lyre* 76]). What was essential to both Australian and American poetic consciousness—the imposing physical landscape, 'large, and without mercy' in Charles Olson's manifesto (Olson 17)—had very different effects. For the Australian poet, writing in a country where 'speech habits come as close to silence as you can get' (*Lyre* 92), 'relief from the chatter of cultured apes' was one thing (32); the Lawrentian 'will to the annihilation of civilised consciousness' (14) quite another. Again, Zwicky's poetry increasingly opens itself to silence, risks the emptiness that might await the poet awaiting a listener.

Writing in 1966, Vivian Smith had regretted that American poetry had had only a marginal influence in Australia, and argued that our ignorance of it only strengthened a 'prevailing conservatism' even among the younger poets (46). What he didn't know was that Donald Allen's groundbreaking collection *New American Poetry* (1960) was by then circulating in Australia and would be a powerful influence on the poets who came to be known as the 'Generation of '68.' In 1979, John Tranter acknowledged in the poetry of John Ashbery, Olson, Frank O'Hara, Gary Snyder,

Robert Creeley, and so on, models for the radical new *l'art pour l'art* modernism that Tranter and his contemporaries were introducing into Australian poetry. They rejected the 'quasi-religious' academic bombast associated, as Tranter saw it, with a moribund Leavisite academic literary studies ('Common Room humanism,' he called it) and set out to instate a 'modernist conception of the poet as a creative artist constructing fictions out of his or her experience in a world qualified by language' (xxv). Zwicky was ten to fifteen years older than most of the Generation of '68, and her academic background and critical leanings aligned her conspicuously with Vincent Buckley and others of the 'metaphysical ascendancy' in Australian literary studies (Docker). Yet in her poetry, too—the poetry of a moralist, as Ivor Indyk insists, and not an aesthete—'everything testifies ... to the shifting and uncertain nature of the ground on which she stands' (Indyk, "Moralist" 46).

For these reasons Zwicky is not a conventional poet of place. Like so many others, her work explores 'the link between the inward movement of the poetic and the specific gravity of place' (Livingston 150), but they are often places in the past or places experienced only in passing: wartime Melbourne, the Java of her early married life, backwoods America, Amsterdam, Jerusalem, Beijing. This mobility makes her sound like a cosmopolitan—that old synonym for a Jew—but in fact, unlike her friend the Canadian-American poet Mark Strand, Zwicky has not felt the need to 'move / to keep things whole' (78). Once in Perth, she made it her home. Her essay 'Neither Out Far Nor in Deep' explores the ways in which both the Swan River, 'that great consoling stretch of water,' and the Indian Ocean 'freed' her 'to meditate': 'My adopted parish handed me the very stuff of poetry ... A little rush of infinity that alters perspective however slightly and briefly permits a standing outside of oneself' (154). It is certainly the case that Perth provided a place from which to write. Zwicky's years in the English Department at UWA were highly productive. In her time there she wrote the majority of her poetry and also her book of essays and criticism, *The Lyre in the Pawnshop* (1986), which is an indispensable companion to the poems. A brilliant, passionate teacher of literature, her practice as a poet and her career in the classroom were mutually informing. Her poems often have pedagogical settings as leaping off points (see, for instance, 'Learning' and 'Charon'), suggesting the importance of her own educational experiences in her artistic formation and her love of teacher-poets such as D. H. Lawrence, who learn in the tutorial room to 'see the other's reality as it exists, regardless of one's own interests, needs and fears' (*Lyre* 7). Her years at UWA were also marked by significant friendships with fellow artist-academics, Dorothy Hewett and Jim Legasse. Hewett and Zwicky are very different poets yet their professional and personal ties were deep and enduring. Legasse's untimely death is dealt with in the powerful sequence 'For Jim, 1947–1986', which ends the final elegiac section of *Ask Me*.

With her trained musician's ear, Zwicky is always listening out for places, for the sounds that can be made or heard only in those places. On the trip to New York in the late 70s she ruminates in her journal on what you need to make the sounds you need to make: 'I suppose I know that change of place isn't likely to change the essential inner voice yet I always have to find out for myself ... The romantic aspirations of America have always attracted me, the alluring language with its vitality and "sauce". I love to hear words spoken' ('Journal' 297–98). Zwicky also has a sharp ear for silences as positive values in poetic form. She is a wonderful exponent of the pauses and flows that can be manipulated in irregular free-verse lines to force us to 'fix our regard exclusively upon' what is being represented (*Lyre* 79). But her poetry is also acutely sensitive to human expression that is outside the range of our hearing. Motifs and images of muffled or silenced sound recur. The image of the submerged piano in 'Isaac Babel's Fiddle' recalls Debussy's submerged cathedral with its drowned bells:

> My first memory of mother playing the piano: Debussy's 'La Cathédrale Engloutie', the buried souls under the ocean waters. I can't remember the legend precisely ... I associated those booming resonances, the grandeur of something tragic and submerged, with my mother herself. ('Journal' 610)

There is also her poem, 'The Caller', about the bronze statue, *Der Rufer* by Gerhard Marcks, standing outside the Art Gallery of WA with its 'dumb cry': 'The mouth yawns open and stays tight and wide like a Greek tragic mask. Poets in this country are excrescent. You can say what you like because nobody listens. Or maybe "hears" is the correct word' ('Journal' 710).

Closely associated with the trope of silenced sound, one of Zwicky's abiding projects is to enable us to hear those who cannot speak, are not conventionally heard, or are not given voice by history, like the minions of the Emperor's Terracotta army. The many animals that find a home in her poetry are a good example of this, as is the brave, unheeded Mrs Noah in the original and striking sequence, 'Ark Voices'. Interestingly, Zwicky stammered as a child and started school late. In conversation she has remarked that she has always had a fear and anxiety of losing her voice, of being unable to speak. The Debussy looms large in this early psychodrama. The silence of those drowned bells is carried over into a line that recurs in her verse: 'true grief is tongueless,' originally in the poem 'Stone Dolphin', much later in 'Aceh' (commissioned in the aftermath of the 2004 Boxing Day tsunami, and which Zwicky was at first reluctant to write), and again 'In Memoriam, JB.'

Zwicky is much concerned with the always forlorn possibility of a dialogue between Australian poetry and its readership. '"Who *is* the poet of today speaking to?" Is there really an audience of whose reality the poet can be sure?' (*Lyre* 57). For her, poetry is always an utterance in search of a response. When it descends into 'a stilted private code addressed to an audience of one' it is doomed. In her writing she seeks the 'organic rhythmical flow of human speech which gives expression to the complexity and fluidity of passion between two people: a speech that keeps pace with the particularities of moment-to-moment existence, a speech that calls up two flesh-and-blood human beings who act in relation to each other' (26). As Zwicky became more and more conscious of listening for a listener (70), the challenges and obscurities of earlier poems and sequences gave way to a poetry in which she is committed to 'plain speech' ('Journal' 719) for its power of initiating 'a dialogue outside of the Self' (*Lyre* 26).

For all that, there are strong continuities between the early and later poems, especially in the quarrelsomeness that Ivor Indyk attributes to Zwicky's Jewish heritage and identity ('Moralist' 34). This, he argues, is the root of her steadfast honesty and characteristic emotional register of isolation (44), and the dramatic intensity and substance of her poetic voice. Other continuities, stylistic and thematic, also persist. Her first collection, *Isaac Babel's Fiddle*, is by turns tender and lyrical, dramatic and satirical. It introduces big themes (mortality, the weight of the past) and displays Zwicky's prodigious learning in its sweeping array of references; yet there are intimate, personal poems, too—about the ways in which a child's drawing refreshes adult eyes, for example ('The Gift'). This command of different modes and a formidable range of cultural references, this enmeshing of the personal with wider concerns, is idiomatic of Zwicky's style throughout her poetry and imbues her work with an earthed, present, and emphatic quality: the sense that things are interconnected in mysterious and subterranean ways.

In Zwicky's work there is also a primal, energetic love of language, which erupts in lists, names, chants, and nursery rhymes. It can be wielded in a most gentle way, as in 'Rhyme for a Granddaughter', or can take the form of what Lisa Gorton has called the 'storm of language' that is 'Kaddish' (48). Sometimes it has an eerie balladic quality (in 'Wolf-Song,' for example, where the influence of Helen Adam can be sensed); often it unfolds into the long lines or long sequences that have some of the expansiveness of Whitman or Ginsberg—a mounting up of repeating sounds and phrases, a cataloguing of peoples and places and things. Of Zwicky's longer sequences, one of her most significant contributions to twentieth-century poetry, Martin Duwell writes perceptively that 'they aim to keep talking before the clouds of silence shut us up' (8).

But never talking for its own sake. For Zwicky, the poet has a job as a social critic. Earlier volumes contain scathing portraits of a particularly odious species of poet-poseur ('The Poet Gives a Reading' and its companion poems), and, like her contemporary Gwen Harwood, her books usually include (indeed, often end with) a satirical tableau of some literary or academic shenanigans, although the satire is always mingled with despair or dismay. Zwicky has never been one to view literature as a profession or take much of an interest in the trappings of literary culture, bemoaning recently in the *Australian Book Review* that at times 'the social-politics of poetry seem to have become a substitute for the art itself' (Zwicky, 'Truth' 56). She is more at home with the notion of the poet as a citizenly and vulnerable witness. Writing in her journal not long before 9/11, she mourns the passing of E. H. Gombrich:

> ... dead at 92—a man whose work I always admired. Austrian Jew whose mother was a pianist and at least once turned pages for Brahms ... Deeply sceptical of collective will he never fell for ideologies that allowed cultural relativism. He distrusted newness for the sake of the new. His best remark (for me) was 'If anybody needs a champion today, it is the artist who shuns rebellious gestures.' You can't be wiser than that. ('Journal' 2137)

The long sense of historical time created with such economy and poignancy in this anecdote reveals a great deal about Zwicky's own past, and especially her grief at the fading away of a whole cultural and intellectual way of being—her way of being. The tribute also shows us how sceptical Zwicky is of the posture of the artist as insurgent. Present here is another kind of artist: unshowy, committed to truth, working slowly and quietly over time like the artisan in 'The Potter,' from *Picnic's* 'Terracotta Army' sequence.

The notes of regret and disillusionment here and elsewhere in Zwicky's later journal entries reflect the insight of an ageing poet, but Zwicky has always worked in an elegiac modality—her greatest poetry comes out of her engagement with abandoned traditions and dead Gods—and it finds mature expression in 'profound elegies and dark love songs' (Adamson 53), including the elegies to her late husband, Karl, in *The Gatekeeper's Wife*, and her elegy for Primo Levi. Wisdom, expressive powers, intellectual curiosity, the yearning after meaning, the instinct for sham: she holds on to their value in the face of a profound sense of cultural and intellectual alienation. This paradox reverberates in late poems such as 'Charon' and 'In Memoriam, JB', and in the journals:

> The world I came from is getting more and more distant, it has practically vanished. That's why I feel the need to bring it alive—not for nostalgic reasons but to remember what went to make the person I am. ('Journal' 1000)

Zwicky's poems are the material record of what made her the person she is, and they revive a personal and historical past through a loving representation of remembered people and events, and old objects and rituals: catching a ride down the street to their house on the running boards of her father's car as he returned from work in 'Afloat'; the 'supine idol' of the chip heater in 'Coming and Going' (see Dougan). The presence and accuracy of these small details function to remind the reader that something of tremendous meaning has almost completely disappeared, and can only be recovered in these vivid images.

The lively quality of much of Zwicky's work (see for instance the beautifully drawn observations of 'Makassar, 1956') draws its energy from such acutely remembered and skilfully chosen autobiographical details. Associative chains of description and imagery connect beneath the surface of the line to a lived life. They are, as it were, at the intersection of what can be found and said again and what is drowned and lost with time.

As Anthony Miller notes, 'Zwicky's poetry is not easy and it is not comfortable, but it is watchful and testing … These are, to adapt a term of praise from Virginia Woolf, poems written for grown-up people' (7). Indeed, there are few such challenging, honest and enduring bodies of work in Australian poetry. As Indyk has precisely observed, Zwicky 'presents the whole human being, in all her aspects, a complicated, contradictory, fallibly-heroic, always surprising individual' ('*Gatekeeper*'). She has always been wary of artists who 'stand aside watching themselves having "feelings"' as opposed to those 'willing to face the reality of [their] own emotions' (*Lyre* 60). Fay Zwicky's *Collected Poems* is a record of just such an artist responding to the twentieth century and turning her attention to the equally difficult and confronting aspects of contemporary life. In her own words, this is poetry that helps the reader 'to bear as well as to see' (60).

Works Cited

Adamson, Robert. 'The Gaze that Kills.' *Australian Book Review* 197 (Dec 1997–Jan 1998): 53.

AustLit. 'Meanjin.' https://www.austlit.edu.au/austlit/page/C277806. Accessed 23 April 2017.

Docker, John. *In a Critical Condition*. Ringwood: Penguin Books, 1984.

Dougan, Lucy. 'Crawling Across Tram Tracks: Extracts from Volumes 5 and 6 of Fay Zwicky's Journal.' *Cordite*. http://cordite.org.au/essays/crawling-across-tram-tracks/. Accessed 23 April 2017.

Duwell, Martin. 'In Positive Voice about the Ultimate Negation.' *The Weekend Australian Review*. (9–10 June 1990): 8.

Gorton, Lisa. Review of Fay Zwicky's *Picnic*. *Australian Book Review* (February 2007): 48.

Indyk, Ivor. 'Fay Zwicky: The Poet as Moralist.' *Southerly* 54.3 (September 1994): 33–50.

Indyk, Ivor. 'Back Cover Citation.' *The Gatekeeper's Wife*. http://www.brandl.com.au/the-gatekeepers-wife/. Accessed 23 April 2017.

Livingston, Robert. 'Glocal Knowledges: Agency and Place in Literary Studies.' *PMLA* 116.1 (January 2001): 145–157.

Miller, Anthony. 'Testing Journey Out of Innocence.' *The West Australian*. (24 March 2007): 7.

Olson, Charles. 'Call me Ishmael.' *Collected Prose*. Eds. Donald Allen and Benjamin Friedlander. Berkeley: University of California Press, 1997.

Schwartz, Larry. 'On the Outside Looking Out.' *The Age*. (4 September 1999): 9

Smith, Vivian. 'Australian Poetry in the '60s: Some Mid-Century Notes.' *Balcony/The Sydney Review* 4 (Southern Autumn), 1966: 46–51.

Strand, Mark. *Collected Poems*. New York: Alfred A. Knopf, 2014.

Tranter, John, ed. *The New Australian Poetry*. St Lucia: Makar Press, 1979.

Tulip, James. 'Kaddish in Two Modern Cultures: The Poetry of Fay Zwicky and Allen Ginsberg.' *Australian Journal of Jewish Studies* 6.2 (1992): 27–35.

Zwicky, Fay. "Border Crossings." *The Best Australian Essays, 2000*. Ed. Peter Craven. Melbourne: Black Inc., 2000. 225–239.

Zwicky, Fay. *Hostages*. Fremantle: Fremantle Arts Centre Press, 1983. [Short stories]

Zwicky, Fay. *The Lyre in the Pawnshop: Essays on Literature and Survival 1974–1984*. Nedlands: University of Western Australia Press, 1986.

Zwicky, Fay. 'Neither Out Far Nor in Deep.' *Lines in the Sand: New Writing from Western Australia*. Eds. Glen Phillips and Julienne van Loon. Swanbourne: The Fellowship of Australian Writers, 2008: 153–156.

Zwicky, Fay. 'The Truth of the Matter.' *Australian Book Review*. (May 2013): 56.

Zwicky, Fay. Unpublished Journal. 13 vols., continuously paginated.

Note on the Text

The text of this edition is based on the following individual collections:

Isaac Babel's Fiddle. Adelaide: Maximus Books, 1975.
Kaddish and Other Poems. St. Lucia: University of Queensland Press, 1982.
Ask Me. St. Lucia: University of Queensland Press, 1990.
The Gatekeeper's Wife. Rose Bay, NSW: Brandl & Schlesinger, 1997.
Picnic: New Poems. Artarmon, NSW: Giramondo, 2006.

Fay Zwicky has made a small number of corrections and minor changes.

All previously uncollected or unpublished poems have been chosen by the poet, and their details of first publication are as follows:

'Bedfellows.' *Rajasthan University Studies in English* 15 (1982–1983): 127. First published as 'Cultures'.
'Madam C.' Previously unpublished (c. 1982).
'Domestic Architecture.' *Family Ties: Australian Poems of the Family*. Ed. Jennifer Strauss. South Melbourne: Oxford University Press, 1998: 141–142.
'A Small Variant on Intelligence.' *A Touch of Ginger*. Applecross: Folio, 1992: 9.
'Primal Dreamcake.' *Fay Zwicky: Poems 1970–1992*. St Lucia: University of Queensland Press, 1993: 173–175.
'Banksia Menziesii.' Epigraph to *Banksia menziesii*. Philippa Nikulinsky. Fremantle: Fremantle Arts Centre Press, 1992. n.p.
'Casting the Die.' *The Sting in the Wattle: Australian Satirical Verse*. Ed. Philip Neilsen. St Lucia: University of Queensland Press, 1993: 147–149.
'The Witnesses.' *Heat* 16 n.s. (2008): 206. First published as 'The Witness'.
'Pages.' *Heat* 18 n.s. (2008): 157–59.
'My Dachshund Schnitzel.' *Heat* 21 n.s. (2009): 7.
'Reasons for Play.' *Westerly* 55.2 (2010): 14–16.
'Charon.' *Australian Book Review* 351 (May 2013): 56.
'Little Fly.' Previously unpublished. October 2014.
'In Rehab.' *Westerly* 59.2 (2014): 208–9.
'Boat Song.' *The West Australian* (5 August 2014): 6.
'Droughtbreaker.' *Griffith Review* 47 (2015): 181.
'In Memoriam, JB.' *Kenyon Review* March/April (2017): 68.

Acknowledgements

We are indebted to Fay Zwicky—her generosity, patience, humour and great knowledge—for helping us bring together these poems.

Special thanks, too, go to Tracy Ryan and John Kinsella.

Thanks to Terri-ann White and team at UWAP for their unwavering support. We also acknowledge Kate McCormack and Madonna Duffy at University of Queensland Press, Veronica Sumegi at Brandl & Schlesinger, and Ivor Indyk at Giramondo for their kind permission to reproduce poems from previously published collections (details on page 11).

Fay Zwicky's essay 'Border Crossings' was first published in *Best Australian Essays 2000*. Ed. Peter Craven. Carlton: Black Inc., 2000: 225–238.

Border Crossings (2000)

Fay Zwicky

I'm often asked, 'How did you become a writer?', a question not easily answered because there are so many mysterious factors involved: temperament, cultural background, historical circumstances, and many more. Although I was born into a Jewish family, my years spent at a Church of England school were equally if not more important to my emotional, intellectual, and moral development. Belonging, if tenuously, to one tradition and yet exposed to the freedoms of a country of transient allegiances, a country where you can re-invent yourself over and over again, where you can invent your community, your own mythology, I was ideally placed to become a story-teller. Whatever the influences determining the course of a life, the directions a writer's work takes will be affected by those cultural and ethical preoccupations and preconceptions with which one individual is saddled, whether present or absent from the stable of origin.

Just as some families destine their sons and daughters for the service of God in monasteries and convents, so my mother destined her children for the service of music. In our household, God was probably Mozart and Bach on good days, and Beethoven when days of wrath were upon us. Worship in the temple of Art is not marked by ethical or moral emphases but by rampant individualism, especially if you were born to run for the lives of Depression-reared parents.

When I was thirty-four years old, my father died and was buried at sea without the proper tribal obsequies: nobody to say Kaddish, the Jewish prayer for the dead, for him, and nobody to throw a spadeful of soil on the coffin. I wasn't present when he died. It happened far away on a ship travelling the Tasman between New Zealand and Australia. At the time, I knew nothing about the Kaddish, which is recited on every regular sabbath day in memory of deceased congregants as well as at the actual funeral service itself.

It is not, as I was to discover, a lament but rather a hymn of praise to God and a celebration of all creation. Although saying Kaddish seems at first acquaintance to be like the Christian ritual of praying for the souls of the dead to speed them through Purgatory, it's not quite the same thing. Purgatory isn't one of Judaism's anticipated torments and Gehenna isn't really the equivalent of hell. It was an actual place near Jerusalem where propitiatory sacrifices used to be made to Moloch, and today is where the ashpits of the town's rubbish dumps stand. The notion of an after-life is less important in Judaic thinking than the memory of the dead retained and honoured by the living survivor.

At the time of my father's death, I knew well enough how to study books but I didn't know how to miss him. His death brought me up against my ignorance of just about everything: ignorance of parenting, ignorance about who, if anyone, one belongs to or wants to belong to, and where, if anywhere, one imagines oneself coming from.

So, against all the rules, I took it upon myself to make amends to him by writing my own 'Kaddish', a long elegy, trying to find a way into what his death meant through the rituals of a religious tradition of which I was an attenuated product, lacking both knowledge and allegiance. Instinct came first. Knowledge came later. Drawing upon traces of the re-discovered wisdom of a tradition, the poem is haunted by layers of ghostly presences, earlier generations of those whose lives went to make a family—with all that such a fallibly heroic enterprise entails. The act of writing the poem was a kind of half-conscious mission to speak up against our mutual obliteration.

When I began writing this poem nine years after my father's death, I didn't know that what the prayer can tell you about familial love, obligation, guilt, and grief is supposed to be spoken only by men. It was a non-Jewish critic who eventually enlightened me as to where authority about family and communal duty belong—invariably and unarguably with the male, the right to speak his sole province. So what about the man unlucky enough to have three daughters and no sons?

To find out more on the subject, I went back to the books and commentaries by various Jewish authorities, and found them, almost without exception, harsh and unyielding, the more so since my experience told me that women had deeper insights into and more sympathy with their fathers, especially those who grew up in an all-female household with a father absent for six years during World War Two. In fairness to the commentators, it should be said that the emphasis tended to fall on the potential for weakening tradition should the female be permitted to speak, rather than on women's inferiority. However, the traditional order of priorities has always rankled with me and continues to do so.

In writing my own 'Kaddish', I turned back half-consciously to very fundamental sources of nurture drawn upon in early childhood: fragments of ritual, nursery rhyme, Biblical lore, all tied in with memories of comfort, anger, shame, and loss. Fragmented memories and isolated images randomly recalled are of no significance in themselves—only the poet's search for meaning within a recognisable context can be of interest. And for this, the poet needs muscles, emotional, spiritual and psychic muscles that transcend the limits of the self. And muscles take time to develop, longer for some than for others.

So, growing up in a family without religious dogma, and the haziest connections with Jewish origins, it was really only the coming of World War Two and the gradual awakening to the fate of Jews in Europe that brought home something of what the religio-cultural meaning of 'being Jewish' was. The sense of being a stranger both to one's own and to one's adopted culture is a familiar theme in Anglo-Jewish writing. I never saw the state of estrangement from mainstream culture as something to be regretted, although I lacked the confidence when young to use its invaluable vantage points. Having one home to know the privileges of exile from is a necessity for a writer, as the work of James Joyce or Henry James can tell you. Having two is a luxury. Given the fact of that remote link with Judaism, it has always seemed surprising that what appeared to have so little substance in the sphere of language, belief, and way of life could have had so much impact on social identity, historical perspectives, and political attitudes.

My father and mother, like both my grandmothers, were born in Australia. Neither they nor I knew Hebrew or Yiddish. I attended the same Church of England school that my mother attended, and we both came top in what used to be called 'Divinity', a subject later to be termed 'Religious Instruction', and eventually to disappear altogether from the curriculum. The first prayer I learned was the Lord's Prayer, which my mother sat on the end of my bed and taught me the day before I started school—though she always denied this. I paid devout attention to the weekly chapel service presided over by the Rev. Townsend who, pinkly illumined by morning sunlight through a fine stained-glass window, radiated an aura of spirituality but who, in retrospect, was pretty thick-witted and had a middling reputation as a cricketer.

On leaving this school, I was presented with the complete works of Shakespeare on austerity rations rice paper. Stamped with the school crest in gold was the daunting motto: *Nisi Dominus Frustra* (without the Lord all is vain). The certificate gummed inside stated your name and the dates you attended school, in my case, 1941–50, the years that saw the bombing of Britain, the Holocaust and the war with Japan. When the school was evacuated to the country, I tasted freedom for the first time but it was not to last. Sent back to Melbourne to have a toe stitched back on after a typical act of disobedience, I was sent to another Church school to get me out of the house, my omniscient mother having made up her mind the Japanese weren't coming after all.

Another motto, another school song. This time, *Vincit qui se vincit* (he conquers who conquers himself). Mottos always implied fruitless struggle whichever way you put the emphasis. Mine fell naturally on *frustra,* knowing full well the meaning of fruitless struggle where my mother was concerned, and, since her wrath was indistinguishable from God's, one didn't tangle willingly with such a parent. The second motto was equally discouraging. What was this self that must be conquered? And was the need to conquer anything what I cared about anyway? Conquest was for the strong of this world, and I was powerless, my outsider status confirmed by the lack of a uniform, a polysyllabic vocabulary, a prodigious piano repertoire and the mystery of Jewish birth.

Given this odd beginning, it's not surprising that it took a long time to find a voice for the buried self, or that I felt diffident about using a ritual when my father died to which I felt barely entitled by upbringing, but to which more atavistic sources compelled me. Back in the 70s I analysed this complex response in an essay entitled, 'Democratic Repression: The Ethnic Strain'. In this essay, I spoke of those authors who helped me find a voice at a time when it needed the sort of sanction the community I lived in didn't provide. These were Jewish-American novelists like Malamud, Saul Bellow and Philip Roth whose work, as I wrote, 'gave me a community I lacked in the Australian context ... The concerns of Australian literature have always appeared essentially solitary, inward-turning, never outer-directed, the babble of speech masking a dumb void; a landscape without a recognisable human being in it.'

From the same essay, I went on to speak of problems encountered in writing the 'Kaddish' for my father:

> I would not have been capable of writing this in Australia ten years ago, so uncertain was I of my identification with the Jewish faith and the legitimacy of its existence in a bland Anglo-Saxon context. Nor would I have dared insert segments of phoneticised Aramaic for fear of revealing that exotic, interloping status of which I was ashamed and afraid ... I felt the burden of those harsh, rasping syllables in the prayer for the dead as a personal penance ... I could not reveal a long-kept secret, say prayers for the dead in my own tongue unless helped to find it.

A breakthrough came with the discovery of Alan Ginsberg's 'Kaddish' for his mother which I came upon seventeen years after it had been published. After reading this long, moving poem, I felt freer to finish my own, less vulnerable about exposing it to public scrutiny in what used to seem an uncomprehending environment. No Australian writer could do this for me, and I went on to describe growing up in this country as 'an exercise in repression'.

While waiting for this breakthrough, I took nourishment where it was available. This came from poetry, from words used precisely, magically and musically. I loved words, their sound, their weight, their capacity to open new worlds. I wanted to use them effectively for they seemed to be my first defence against powerlessness. The source of my first serious acquaintance with poetry came from the hymns we sang every morning at assembly, the words sometimes very fine and other times utterly banal. George Herbert and William Blake rubbed shoulders with Edward Grubb and Percy Dearmer in our battered blue hymn books, but the combination of words and rousing music never failed to inspire a sense of well-being. We didn't always know exactly what we were singing about, but the music carried us along. For example, 'There is a green hill far away *without* a city wall.' If there was no wall, why was it necessary to mention the fact that it wasn't there? It took quite a few years before the real meaning sank in.

Another misunderstanding involved the word 'aweful' as in 'Let all your lamps be bright/ And trim the golden flame/ Gird up your loins as in his sight/ For aweful is his name.' Wasn't it meant to be a song of praise? Why did it seem to damn the Almighty? Just one more of those mysteries language set out to trap us in. Like those shame-making mispronunciations when required to read aloud in class, like 'misled' and 'awry', that one never heard uttered in everyday conversation.

The hymns I liked best were not about God directly but about nature. I obviously hadn't tapped these hymns' original sources in the Psalms which are full of imagery from the natural world. The one I liked best was a hymn ascribed to St Patrick and it was called, enigmatically, St Patrick's Breastplate:

> I bind unto myself today
> The virtues of the starlit heaven,
> The glorious sun's life-giving ray,
> The whiteness of the moon at even,
> The flashing of the lightning free,
> The whirling wind's tempestuous shocks,
> The stable earth, the deep salt sea,
> Around the old eternal rocks.

There was also a bit of plainsong, supposed to be by St Francis of Assisi, translated by Matthew Arnold, which had a wonderful line, the only one I can remember: 'Praisèd be my Lord God for our sister Water: who is very serviceable unto us and humble and precious and clean.' Brother Fire was 'mighty and strong' and the stars were set 'clear and lovely' in heaven, which seemed cosmically reassuring in every way.

Coming from a home of some turbulence, I liked the bare simplicity and meditative stillness of the Sarum Primer of 1558. It seemed to offer a safe passage through a stormy world from beginning to end, but I hadn't yet learned to question anything about belief when I took its simple lines to heart:

> God be in my head,
> And in my understanding;
> God be in my eyes,
> And in my looking;
> God be in my mouth,
> And in my speaking;
> God be in my heart,
> And in my thinking;
> God be at mine end,
> And at my departing.

The same need for peace in the awful upheavals of adolescence drew me to Miss Russell, my Quaker teacher who, sensing a troubled child, took me to the Quaker meeting house on Sundays where I encountered a productive silence for the first time in my life. It was from teachers like Miss Russell with her gentle voice and soothing kindness (she was extremely deaf) that I drew strength to help me overcome my fear and self-consciousness. I will never forget her intuitive tact in dealing with troubled young souls and I'm sure her Quaker affiliation had much to do with her pacific and unintrusive nature. It struck me as remarkable that, very late in her life, she married the Jewish art master at Geelong Grammar, a refugee from Hitler's Germany, and, although they didn't have long together, I'm sure they were able to nourish each other.

It was Miss Russell who taught me that to reflect wasn't simply an affair of the intellect and the will, but a gentler form of receptiveness. Her wisdom instilled the notion of a conscience, a social awareness of a wider morality that was never moralistic. Her quiet voice spoke louder to me than all the fervent injunctions addressed stridently at home, from pulpits of all denominations, and sometimes in the classroom. Channelling my natural sympathy for the poor and oppressed into creative paths, she gave me translations of classical Chinese poetry to read, and encouraged me to write and read poetry without feeling freakish.

There was no music in the Quaker meeting house, but the more energetic side of my nature was to find satisfaction in the grand martial rhythms of Mrs Julia Ward Howe's 'Battle Hymn of the Republic' with its promise of vengeance on an Old Testamental scale, the letting loose of destructive forces for mankind's betterment:

> Mine eyes have seen the glory of the coming of the Lord;
> He is trampling out the vintage where the grapes of wrath are stored;
> He hath loosed the fateful lightning of his terrible swift sword:
> His truth is marching on.

And this rousing revolutionary vision is followed by a graphic picture of soldiers huddling in encampments during the American Civil War that stirred my liberationist sympathies, and turned me eventually into a radical supporter of the oppressed and the enslaved:

> I have seen him in the watch fires of a hundred circling camps;
> They have builded him an altar in the evening dews and damps;
> I have read his righteous sentence by the dim and flaring lamps:
> His Day is marching on.

And, finally, at Easter, my need to share the pathos of the Crucifixion and identify with the rebel underdog found full and tearful outlets in sad hymns with solemn, funereal chorale music by J. S. Bach. As for example in:

> O sacred head sore wounded,
> Defiled and put to scorn,
> O kingly head surrounded
> With mocking crown of thorn.

The fate of the outsider who suffered multiple humiliations at the hands of the mainstream was uppermost in my garbled imagination, my sympathies always directed to the noble despised figure of the One who was Different in both life and literature. Mindful of my own early humiliations at the hands of the majority, I understood in my bones what it was like to feel and be thought stupid, the outsider with a lot on her mind and a weight on her heart like a guilty secret. So there were two kinds of education going on at home and at school. I took from each an enjoyment of and curiosity about the outside world which no amount of difficulty could quench, and for this I have to be grateful to the freedom to think that my parents and my education gave me, enabling me to cross borders without fear and to relish difference, to acquire the tools necessary in learning to discipline and shape the sprawl of raw temperamental protoplasm, and to avoid getting stuck in obsessional states of mind.

I've spoken so far about certain aspects of traditional rituals encountered prior to the development of consciousness, contacts charged with inescapable attitudes and values that have fed the poet's imagination. But what happens when these attitudes and values absorbed in childhood come under intellectual scrutiny? How does the writer deal with the question of belief?

As a child of the 1930s and 40s, I was brought up to be suspicious of abstractions, to be wary of easy consolations, to be sceptical of any ideology or theology purporting to offer solutions. Growing up in wartime, my generation was trained early to be alert to language's betrayals, obliged to bury the natural hunger of the young for miraculous revelation. Consequently, the religious impulse unmediated by reason has always made me uneasy. I'm pretty sure that my stroppy obsession with precision and accuracy in the use of language has at least part of its genesis in this growing up during the Second World War, a historical accident for which I've always been grateful. As Miroslav Holub the poet has said when comparing the beady-eyed attention we paid language with today's clichéd blur: 'Everything seemed so important, every image, every metaphor seemed to matter in a special way.'

Whether because one's senses are sharpened during childhood and times of crisis or because one's father suddenly disappeared for six crucial years, those early childhood years were the source of most potent memories. Across painstaking letters dispatched with poignant regularity from Borneo, Brunei, Moratai, Tarakan, Balikpapan was stamped the warning imprint, 'Careless Talk Costs Lives'. The impact of that cryptic message was to be felt far more deeply in my future work than I could possibly have realised at the time.

Back in our Australian provincial classrooms we studied examples of wartime propaganda, despising the rhetoric of nationalism and conceptually aerated adjectives like 'glorious', 'invincible', 'omnipotent', weighing up the approval, disapproval, and neutrality ratings of columns of synonyms: 'I am firm. You are obstinate. He is pig-headed.' While being alerted to the manipulative powers of language, I was manipulating myself into linguistic paralysis, scrupulous to the point of schizophrenic self-distrust. To this day, when confronted with an adjective implying judgment, I still mentally shift through those old gradations of approval to mild disapproval right across the spectrum to strong disapproval in order to reach a fair conclusion and to get as close to the truth of the matter as possible. Very ethical, very idealistic, but hard on the imaginative life and the notion of spontaneous utterance.

As undergraduates, we read existentialist philosophers, believed in free will, and took personal responsibility for our actions. The writers I most admired were European dissidents, starting with Nietzsche and Kierkegaard, who displayed stoic courage, steely irony, an unsmiling moral strenuousness cut off from religious affiliation. Writers who came later like Malraux, Koestler, Camus, Sartre, Orwell, represented freedom from prejudice and superstition. They emerged from the landscape of a war that took our fathers from home, writers inseparable from the apparatus of totalitarianism, the concentration camps, Nazism and Stalinism. Austere, tough, angry about social injustice, these were writers in whose work the notion of commitment to human solidarity was foremost, who raged against the dying of the light, and who, by testifying to the violence and futility of contemporary history, manage, in spite of everything, to keep faith and hope alive in the Western humanist legacy of art, literature, at least acknowledging if not accepting the legitimacy of Judeo-Christian religious tradition. The cranky moral earnestness of the Melbourne of my youth comprising a kind of stern Leftist didacticism coupled with the muscular Protestantism of my Church of England schooling slotted easily into the cultural and political upheavals that animated my literary heroes.

I'm not sure in what sense these early concerns of my world could be called 'religious'. Cultural and ethical maybe, but not necessarily spiritual, surely a necessary component of the religious sensibility. Passionate dissent is sometimes confused with religious inclination in this country, a kind of stroppy dissatisfaction with what this earth has to offer, and certainly my own writing seems to have depended for a long time on remaining adversarial, as if needing the skewed vantage point of isolation from which to maintain creative rage against injustice.

I suppose the notion of spirituality is a bit fraught for me because, as popularly understood, it implies a bloodless, ascetic rejection of the physical world, and a disembodied religiosity that leave poetry and female experience out in the cold. So I'm sceptical of any system that divorces apprehension of the numinous from the life of the senses. It's not unusual for a writer keyed in early childhood to the rhetoric of prayer and chant to be capable of shifting easily between mundane recrimination and transcendence in later life. Emily Dickinson describes this duality of poetic understanding as the most natural way of being imaginable, especially in a poem called 'This world is not Conclusion':

> This world is not Conclusion.
> A Species stands beyond—
> Invisible, as Music—
> But positive, as Sound—
> It beckons, and it baffles—
> Philosophy—don't know—
> And through a Riddle, at the last—
> Sagacity, must go—
> To guess it, puzzles scholars—
> To gain it, Men have borne
> Contempt of Generations
> And Crucifixion, shown—
> Faith slips—and laughs, and rallies—
> Blushes, if any see—
> Plucks at a twig of Evidence—
> And asks a Vane, the way—
> Much Gesture, from the Pulpit—
> Strong Hallelujahs roll—
> Narcotics cannot still the Tooth
> That nibbles at the soul—

That tooth nibbling at the soul is known to all moralists and seekers of the Puritan persuasion, easily crossing denominational borders. Few poets have been able to dramatise the working of the mind scrutinising its motives so effectively. These most concrete metaphors illuminate the authenticity of her understanding of the meaning of faith far better than abstract instructions from pulpits.

Much of what has appealed to me in past brushes with religious experience has, in fact, been paradoxically removed from the physical world, its very bodylessness something of a relief from the burden of the flesh and its assorted mischiefs. I associate this relief with language—the mysteries of the language of prayer, the poetry of the Psalms and the Prophets, the differing narrative styles of the Old Testament and the Gospels, the formalities of ritual, the repetitive comfort of well-known liturgical structures absorbed unconsciously in childhood. To a child with an obedient, sensitive ear, the alternation of language levels from very simple everyday usage for the purpose of introspective meditation, through to the formal magniloquence of scriptural invocation celebrating major events in the ecclesiastical calendar, provided an invaluable training ground for the nurture and development of a poet.

I may be chronologically remote from my childhood and yet its simpler concerns are still very present. I feel very little different from the child who once took delight in the idea of Aaron's rod causing water to spring from the rock in the desert. Nor do I feel a whit less sympathetic to Job's dilemma than I did as an eleven year old deputed to write the Morality play for our primary school's enactment of a medieval fairground. True to a lifetime preoccupation with the question of undeserved suffering, I chose the nearest story I could find in the Bible to a tragic drama. Although the script of that early effort no longer exists, I remember the buzz I got from devising cheeky lines for the Devil's interview with God, and from working up a lather on Job's behalf.

Writing this play marked the beginning of my conscious opposition to the God of the Bible. I found myself much readier to invest Job with a tragic hero's resistance to and complaint about the disasters that befell him than I was in coming to terms with a God bent on testing Job's endurance with such monstrous indifference. I certainly wasn't able to accept the idea that the servant of God should suffer willingly in order that others may be improved. I couldn't come at it when I was eleven and I still find his submission troubling even though I'm less likely to say so with such defiance: too many things have happened since those clays of heedless bravado.

At one point, you may remember Job says:

Though he slay me, yet will I trust in Him;
But I will argue my ways before Him.
This also shall be my salvation,
That a hypocrite cannot come before Him.

In these lines, it seemed to me that Job rose to inspirational heights, equally matched in his debate with God. But once God had spoken, Job gave away his swagger, his sublime defiance—

Wherefore I now abhor my words, and repent,
Seeing I am dust and ashes.

I have to admit I cheated on the original, refusing to have my hero abase himself in what seemed a craven way before God's harsh rebuke:

Behold, I am of small account; what shall I answer Thee?
I lay my hand upon my mouth.

I was ready in those days to back tragedy's capacity to glorify human resistance to necessity. Prometheus defied Zeus with all stops out—why should Job not be allowed the same spiritual flare before extinction? Because Job belongs to the submissive Hebrew tradition and Prometheus to the intellectual hubris of the Greek. Tragedy is only possible to a mind which is agnostic since there can be no compensating hereafter for a tragic hero. Less defiant today, I'm more likely to lay a hand over my mouth before putting the tragic foot in it. However, I began as an agnostic and an agnostic I remain, a stake in both the Hebrew and Greek traditions, too much of a Jew to be a Christian, too Christian to be much of a Jew.

Poetry has always seemed to me a source of hope, a means of speaking against any orthodoxy, be it religious, political, or social. It has offered a place for the dissenting imagination that hankers to encompass not only the truth of what is, what has been, but what might be or what might have been.

In the pages of my journal, kept over many years, the following passage from 1995 occurs:

> The Psalms have given me the most inspired comfort. But is it just a trick of language or do I actually take hold of something in the act of reading? Some sustaining force behind the words, the voice of the fallible human seeking redemption in a crazy act of faith in an unseen being. 'I am like a pelican of the wilderness; I am like an owl of the desert. I watch and am as a sparrow alone upon the house top.' The imagery is very poignant and feels right.

In the same engaging way, the poems of the seventeenth-century parson-poet of Bemerton, George Herbert, modest and radiantly illuminating about his inner conflict, have the familiar pull between the attractions of the world and the call to renounce it. Underneath it all, there is true belief in the One to whom he speaks as familiarly as to a mortal friend, his source of strength and survival. He's willing to go all the way with whatever God ordains whether he's 'cast down' or afforded help:

> I will complain, yet praise;
> I will bewail, approve;
> And all my sowre-sweet days
> I will lament and love.

That just about says it all: sour-sweet days. The state of exile is relative and it would appear that Herbert felt just as cut off in his village parish as I feel out of

God's earshot on the remotest edge of this continent. We both received our sense of God from the stern, fallible beauty of the King James Version's resonant prose. It's an old infatuation, and even now I can't tell how much of its impact depended on the means of expression rather than what was actually being expressed.

There is an epigraph to a recent autobiographical memoir by the now-deceased young professor of philosophy at London University, Gillian Rose. The book is called *Love's Work,* and the epigraph is taken from an eighteenth-century Kabbalist called Staretz Silouan. It reads, 'Keep your mind in hell, and despair not.' Taken together with Herbert's poem, I believe it offers a kind of answer to Job. I'm grateful to both of them. After all, keeping afloat, keeping one's spiritual stamina intact even in hell, seems a not unreasonable aim for ageing agnostics.

ISAAC BABEL'S FIDDLE

Perspective

1954:
There were the hours we spent
In gentle wonderment, walking together.
Shadows of the afternoon across our path,
Yet we were blinded by a greater sun, made
One and still divided in burning clarity of
Self, souls suspended in the bright air.
We were grave lovers, engulfed as by a mighty
Swell of tears; the pressure of the hand, the
Tender eyes, the whole merged in a whole, yet
You could speak—I was afraid to yield the
Vastness to a word, a sign that might trouble
The hour, the brightness and the joy.
We were grave lovers (you promised this would be
Although I doubted); our laughter grew
To a brave thing. So rare a day as this
We did not know would end so soon whose
Night was but the ashes of our noon.

1974:
I am supposed to blench for you, my heightened
Friend who loved. Miss R. who showed (said Bernard
C., whoever he) 'cold purity of passion' but
'Added neither weight nor roused new hope thereby
For undergraduate poetry.' He knew his stuff.
He knew that 'burning clarity of self' was just
A blind, that wholes cannot grammatically (or
Any other way) be merged in wholes, that the
Existence of a soul was doubtful (Donne be damned)
In Melbourne of the Fifties. But calloused to
Survive, though he she loved is dead and she was
In another country burning laid, I wouldn't change
A word, young fuzzy platonist, whose fine illusory
Clarity throughout less heightened years has unmade
Me.

Survival Kit

I have waited to be forty all my life (always a
Sucker for precise reckoning), and
Here is the year beckoning me
To be where I always wanted, legitimately.
Dieu et mon droit, a confirmation devoutly
Wished for, a mark on the census that I am beginning
Where I began, that nothing has been worth winning,
That nothing has definitely been won,
Or absolutely lost.
                         Heart's death old hat,
Mine has died time and again tending experience,
Absurd handmaiden to the absurd, removing my glasses
At movies, chickening on violence even at one remove,
Moping with Mahler, weak for my children, lead
Bleater of *Kindertotenlieder*, forestalling world's
End on the end of a pin, fraught with quibble and
Linguistic tic, pernickety ironic nit-picking
Academic.
                        Bound to admit that I
Welcome the end of a world that I am, I rejoice
In the worm drinking dew, the lift as the leaf
Bursts its bud, gaiety in grief.
                        Attitudes crumble.
The heart survives in bumbling triumphal shouts and
Giggles—in night skies, in the babble of birds,
Grass murmurs, bravura of rocks. So who mourns
Despair, anguish, fury, passion, fallen away
Painlessly as another year's petals? Did the
Nightingales carrying on in the woods of Mycenae
Give a damn for Agamemnon?

An Australian

(Self-Portrait by Clifton Pugh)

Before you buy your ticket, loose the
Atrophy of caste (white, skilled, and for
Ten quid you can, you can burn the pianola,
Galoshes, mum, and that inner man she hangs
About with) before, I say, look well at this
Visible man, his holy frugal ghost.
They keep strange company. Poised between
Camps, you think he's free to pitch and fend,
Speculate and prophesy. You're wrong. He keeps
His end up by a tight-rope walker's trick,
Erectile stance, trial upon trial of fine
Adjustment in the austere shell of his curls,
Fronted by fall upon fall, a trunkless
John the Baptist, spectacled. Wordless
In a dumb landscape, sardonic, fretful, nurses
A faulty prospect without complaint.
Centaur in collage, below the belt he keeps
A flaccid rooted poise, knocks romantic cliché
In his groin-rumpled shorts, granite legs; clenched
Granite hand guards dying energies.
                        Spectre to himself, the cloudless
Sky, the casual rocks, the sated sun, the broken camp;
Now are you game to plant your belly in that sun?

To a Sea Horse

The male has a pouch on the underside of the tail into which the female injects the eggs. When the eggs hatch it looks as if the male is giving birth to the young. Even after hatching, the young remain near the father, darting back into his pouch if danger threatens.

Wall-eyed snouter, sweet feeble translucent
Tiny eunuch teetering on your rocker,
Pouting, corseted in
Rings of bone, flesh flaps
Fanning the tides as you totter and roll
Forward, but never so forward as
She.
Flex your pipes for the winter.
Keep an upright house.
Pucker piped lips for her, flex,
Flex your rings, flash your fin
If you can, man. Watch it!
Your love's bearing down with
Transparent efficiency, that
Abrasive lady's been starching her
Dorsal for meeting, nudges
Neatly your ring-tailed poise;
Totter and flex, finny vibrato for
Sex (can't afford to go off your
Rocker at this stage),
FLEX!
Chess knights collide:
A shuddering pouchful of eggs.
Nuzzle your snouters, sweet
Sons and daughters, tip to
Your tiny transparencies,
Hatched in your warmth,
Flexed in your strength.
They'd be mad to trust women
After this.

Isaac Babel's Fiddle Reaches the Indian Ocean

'Mr. Zagursky ran a factory of infant prodigies, a factory of Jewish dwarfs in lace collars and patent-leather pumps. He hunted them out in the slums of Moldavanka, in the evil-smelling courtyards of the Old Market ... My father decided that I should emulate them ... I was fettered to the instruments of my torture, and dragged them about with me ... One day I left home laden like a beast of burden with violin-case, violin, music, and twelve roubles in cash—payment for a month's tuition. I was going along Nezhin Street; to get to Zagursky's I should have turned into Dvoryanskaya but instead of that I found myself at the harbour ... So began my liberation.'

Isaac Babel: Awakening

Just try and cast a piano
In the sea
Romantically.
Take it from me, you'll
Never make it.

I tried it once
Or twice. My
Polished albatross
Kicked me as we
Sank through
Coral gardens.

And rose, rosewood
Bird and I,
Buoyed by
Bubbling spirals past
The emerald gills,
The darting purple fins,

Up through the silent
Gardens beckoning
In dappled solar tracks
To break the
Limpid bounds of an
Elysium aquamarine.

What happened when you left
That day? A day of frozen
Lakes and weighted birches,
Fleeing mittenless
The fond solicitude
That sealed your case

And thrust you talentless
Upon Zagursky's stoop to
Sit among the drooping
Ugly boys, your eyes
Intent upon their
Bruised necks, their neat

Doll's feet; Anchises' tadpoles
In withered velvet suits
Bearing their father, *theotokoi*,
Upon their bows to
101st street, East, the
Summerhearted phoenix land.

You'd seen your father
Touch his cap and bow
While Cossacks tore
His store apart.
Meanwhile your heart
Quickened with Dumas,

Stopped with Turgenev
(Disguised by Sevcik
On the stand). It was your
Judashand that flung the
Fiddle, spent the rouble
For Zagursky's care into

Odessa's sandbar—whose voice
Did you obey that day you
Sounded out the waterfront?
Hydrophobic shoot of land-locked
Scholars, febrile storekeepers
And gaunt Iberian rabbis in their caves.

The milling port that
Catapulted Heifetz, Elman
From the Tsarevitch's sight
Kept you, boy and man apart,
Heir to a single
Season of the heart.

You had no need to join
A brutal company;
(The world's a Cossack haunt
In any case—Turgenev
Might have told you *that*),
What did you prove,

Master of silence? That you
Could pass the test
Your father failed, autumnal friend?
The silent salty wastes
Await us. These (and *they*)
Will get us in the end—meantime

The tendrils of the sea
Most tenderly embrace the
Adamantine gloss,
Time's rivulets are filtered,
Harmless, through each curled eyelet,
Every key is stilled.

The final feathered clamp
And suck of blind anemones
Rock the ancestral fate to jar
A host of ghostly swimmers,
Measuring their buoyant gravity
Beyond Odessa's black sandbar.

In Memory of Ries Mulder

(1909–1973)

Seeing the coming storm, tired of the way,
You drew to sleep. Rest quiet, Ries, who
Painted, talked, was loved by friends who
Fled the north and cannot bury you.
Blood in a lung, the new admitted guest
Sat in your room till we had gone, to
Swell his nightmare sac. An easy tender
Host, you gave yourself in gently
Angled prow suspended on an opalescent
Calm, painted when we were young
In Java.
How still it was. The red sun sank
Behind the spire, fired the canal and
Died. We drank to our next meeting,
Raised a glass against your subtle
Patient guest and ours. The sun's shaft
Struck the prow, shattered the summer
Waterscape one fiery time and charged a
Common autumn day with fear. You knew.
We set our faces light with expectation
(Time on our side, young in the south)
On a meeting: 'Seven years? Of course
We'll make it.'
Dear failed and gifted friend, the wind
Has blown us all to the earth's end never
To cross that sea again.
But on the clear cerulean wave your
Young and steadfast prow will rock
Itself asleep for ever.

Ijsselstein

For Anna

This is your friendly pelican
Talking to you, just above your ear:
The seas all rush together
As you chomp and snort among
My feathers. Burrow your
Pulsating skull against me,
Scan your larder well and choose
Your fill today, dear small predator,
Scrabbling to be free. Tomorrow,
With your trusting breath and
Reckless gums you shall devour
The world. And me.

Orpheus

As at a sign you'll go and no more
Turn. Night's window starred with warning
Runway markers opens: the plane waits.
Solemn boy again, I took your case with
Love, pity—books, you said, just books,
The squirrel hoard, the refuge, chosen
Cage. Our light affectionate irony
Played between the bars deceiving none
But us. Trapped migratory birds
More reckless of their years would
Probe a prison no more gentle—their
Simple islands lie in the sun and
Do not move. Our quicksand havens shift
To outstay the gnawing tides of love.

The Name of the Game

John Donne, who are you kidding?
' ... nor yet canst thou kill me.'
                    Fine words.
Ah, fine fine words to gird the heart,
To brush me for a minute to infinity.
But back I come. And so did you, be
Honest now.
                    Each night
I tell him in the sink, tell him
Scouring the floor on his black back:
Get the hell out of my kitchen!
I'm not ready for you yet and
When I am I'll do the taking.
Fine literary stance, poor heir to
Papa Ernest (poorer comforter than you).
But at the small pale root
That bound me long before I read a book
A swelling starts, a dark flower
Opens waxen leaves—no poppy this,
Dear John Chrysostomos.
                    The voice of wax
Tells me the taker's name
And I (and you) believe it.

Respite

Ay, many flowering islands lie
In the waters of wide Agony.
                              Shelley

Skeined and scented shore,
Spray drifts in piney whiffs
Suspended in sunlight.

Our moon-light thongs skim
The monotonous delicacy
Of skeletal shells,

Shallow fragile island
Sand, you on Rottnest,
I in Hydra. '*Hudra*',

Corrects Nick the God giving
My son a short back-and-sides
In Nedlands, assimilating him

Head first into the land
Of short back-and-sides,
Paving his track while I'm

Away on Hydra: *you* are
Always where you are,
Easy heir to lake and mountain

Bleak with guilt and tamed
By God. And on this guiltless
Strand you too are guiltless:

Unpilgrim'd fragile earth,
Where is my absolution?
Comical wife in a pink hat

Looking for what? A world
In a grain of sand when a
Grain of sand is a grain

Of sand (so they tell me
In this straightened land:
His name *is* Theos, I didn't invent

Him, and he has a son,
An Aristotle or a Plato, also
With short back-and-sides).

'Hudra has no cars, many tourists;
No, I have no wish to return.
Not yet.' When his and my son

Greet the scented sand
Will they touch Rottnest or
Must my shoot propitiate

The Hydran gods for ever?
Have crisp white minutes
In a Nedlands barber's chair

Refused to chill the
Chafing ghost? Yet drowned
Beneath the turquoise-purple

Bowl of bay, lashed
With fine white streamers,
Stroked with sunlight,

Cruelly triumphantly unshriven
I am spent in you, the gods no more
Than distant thunder at a feast.

The Gift

Today I thought she gave me
Back the eyes I'd lost.
Contained and tough, painted
An elephant, trunk
Ecstatically reared,
Feet set fast

In a field of spiky grasses
Trees. Above, birds of red,
Green, purple and orange hang
In fine suspense. Equidistant
Careless and serene they loop
A tranquil sky.

Primed by his clenched unshaking
Creator, the earless beast
Bellows her triumph to the stars.
Quickened, I'm thrust to earth,
Pulsed by the ebbing riot of
My child's making.

Emily Dickinson Judges the Bread Division at the Amherst Cattle Show, 1858

I   *Volume*

Here is bread:
      not more nor less than what you see,
It asks for mercy—I am God to give—
Stands as I stand (armoured, gleaming white
Behind my muslin smile, grand upon
The sweetness of this fearful day),
Waits on my step, my virgin adversary, life
Unflinching whole, upon a weathered bench
Pleading a tiny pellet of justice.
Of *me*!
      Reaper or victim, so far the act is fine;
Pastor Jenkins' nose approves my draped humility
But cannot smell my pride—I shine
Upon his coat behind a smile.
Yes, there is Bread:
      and I am where I am,
Winged, decorous, stony-hearted captive judge;
Nobody dare befriend me.

II   *Texture*

Moonscape sways, the crested craters yawn
Under my knife, propitiating sabbath stroke:
         My father's economic vestal,
He would eat no bread but mine, contractor
For my crumb, his own communicant forever
Wrapped about a stone.
Votaries rebuffed resume, their crowns awry,
The silvered lacey cells; and God marks
Time, awaits the silken even grain.
         Today
Your starving eaglet breaks pitted bread
With sparrows—no question of friendship.
         But is't for this
I'll go, strangling in smiles, to heaven?
Mourn the eagle, mourn the sparrow,
Pastor can you? Test the crater's rim for me,
Shelter my responsibility beneath your
Tight black coat—here,
Here is the knife!
A healthy crust but I suspect
Surfeit of saleratus.

III   *Aroma*

         I cut, cut, cut,
My culprit dies in my wrath.
Wafted by bells on his winged collar
Rises, buoyed by sweet wraiths
Into fine new air.
         Strutting
In yeasty quicksands I send him at last,
About my neck the acid victor's wreath,
My smile stuck fast.
         Amherst's pigeons
Ponder the sourness in the air.

IV   Colour

White is the colour of tribulation
White is the antimacassar of my cell
White is the inexorable collar
White is the dealer's hand
White the entrenched priestess.

Full marks.

Lear, Class '71

Trendy misses
In your gypsy dresses
Combing down your
Images of death,
*Today's theme is
Renunciation*:
Violets dwindle
On your breath,
Sunlight lilts upon
Your hair. *Look, will
You a moment at the
Sequence of suffering ...
Have you, Miss Hardcastle,
Another word for it?
Avoid it, then, by
All means—the
Rest of you
Take
Note.*
Miss Hardcastle's father,
Bauxite magnate, knows
Never to give away:
(a) lands
(b) knights
(c) retainers for:
To be powerless
Invites
Attack.
He countenanced violence
In the nursery; Miss
Hardcastle orders her fear
With a moral, and young
Mr Middleton there, wandering
In the meadows of her hair
Yields to
Formal justice.

As they (and you) grow older
Your teachers will become
Somewhat evasive
On the subject, resort to
Delicate stratagems
To give the iron ball a miss,
To skip the rack, to pare
The teeth of:
Serpent
Vulture
Tiger
Bear
Wolf
Kite and,
Need I remind you,
Dog, coiled
In the obedient mind,
Images merely.
'Microcosm of the Human Race'—
Regrettable overstatement but
One suggestive of profound
Truth to be:
Defined
Analyzed
Expanded
Qualified
For next
Week.
To suffer ripeness,
If it come,
Extends at present
Beyond the bounds of
Your curriculum and
The Administration
Chooses to
Grant us
No Extension.

Catullus at Sirmio

Time to speak well of the dead—who
Better than I, hunched on a
Rise in the delicate snows above
Garda whirling in crested froth.
My bleaching eye welcomes the skiff
Dancing to the whipping Dolomite blast
Between solemn pleasure boats,
Perfututa futata. They are coursing to
Riva, Malcesine, Desenzano chock with
Men, women like armchairs pink
Northerners frozen and stuffed, grasping
The coast pitched aghast from the
Curling steeps and hollows.
With reason.
Their owners are responsible men who
Threaten their captains regularly;
Perfututa futata, the asses are riding
Unpredictable waters.
I assure you that safety was never my
First consideration: my dervish sail
Rose to the crags of Dalmatia, the Cyclades
Hissing in oil to the violent Pontic, the
Lulling the lapping Pontic (O
Lesbia defututa futata!) and
O it is a cold day when pleasure
Hugs the dark coast.
     Giggling spirochetes twirl
Through the alleys of Rome, the lesbians,
Faggots, the whole jigging tribe of Clodii
Perfututa futata, I cooked them and ate
Them for supper agitating old stiffening
Cicero preparing his last case.

Spinoza's Lens

Baruch—ah, Benedict (best of both worlds and worst),
Who taught Elijah's chariot its place,
Squeezing the scriptural bubble until it burst

And shredded in the furred Sanhedrin's face.
Smart boy! He's learnt some names. Now he can talk
Of Descartes, Kepler, Galileo—words
As even his father can't pronounce. The chalk
Descends with violence: from the burning bush rise birds.

Fledged, forged, reviled
In this intemperate school,
Whose infinite indifference kept
Your buoyant pessimism cool?

Summer Pogrom

Spade-bearded Grandfather, squat Lenin
In the snows of Donna Buang.
Your bicycle a wiry crutch, nomadic homburg
Alien, black, correct. Beneath, the curt defiant
Filamented eye. Does it count the dead
Between the Cossack horses' legs in Kovno?

Those dead who sleep in me, me dry
In a garden veiled with myrtle and oleander,
Desert snows that powder memory's track
Scoured by burning winds from eastern rocks,
Flushing the lobes of mind,
Fat white dormant flowrets.

Aggressive under dappled shade, girl in a glove;
Collins Street in autumn,
Mirage of clattering crowds: Why don't you speak English?
I don't understand, *I don't understand!*
Sei nicht so ein Dummerchen, nobody cares.
Not for you the upreared hooves of Nikolai,
Eat your icecream, Kleine, *may his soul rot,*
These are good days.

Flared candles; the gift of children; love,
Need fulfilled, a name it has to have—how else to feel?
A radiance in the garden, the Electrolux man chats,
Cosy spectre of the afternoon's decay.
My eye his eye, the snows of Kovno cover us.
Is that my son bloodied against Isaac the Baker's door?

The tepid river's edge, reeds creak, rats' nests fold and quiver,
My feet sink in sand; the children splash and call, sleek
Little satyrs diamond-eyed reined to summer's roundabout,
Hiding from me. Must I excavate you,
Agents of my death? Hushed snows are deep, the
Dead lie deep in me.

Song of Experience

The tasteful landau rolls it course
Discreetly grey, the pusher's wrist applies
The new-born knack, swoops on the curb to
Surge, primed with mysterious rites of
Fluent and felicitous resource.
Anchored upon his back the infant
Gravely sweeps the cushioned world,
Freckled by tender endless leaves, the
Crenellated mottlings of summer's breath;
Slyly unfurled, an eye describes the ageless
Promenade, imprints a lightning presence on the sky
And briefly renders down his graven death.

And Innocence?

The light spins out against your drowsy lids
Your craft is manned,
Pulsed by your dreaming halcyon heart,
By summer spanned

You roll. Though fretful tracings of the sun
Divert your sight
Your space probe purges earth
Of day and night.

Unwhorled, unpoled, unpressed to qualify
Your sleeping breath,
Your supine flight, inviolate stunt man, yet
Unbriefed for death.

Gall Tripartite

I   Cold Ham for Sigmund

Heriger, bishop of Mainz, saw a prophet who said he had been carried off to hell. Among other details, he revealed that hell was surrounded by dense woods. To this, bishop Heriger replied with laughter: 'In that case I'll send my swineherd to that grazing ground and get him to take my thin pigs with him.'

From the MS of St Augustine

The clever cleric knows the rules,
A recognized authority
On all the grids and cul-de-sacs
Of limbo, hell and purgatory.

Good citizens of Mainz rejoice
That Heriger is in the chair!
If what you thought was hell today
He'll let you know it wasn't there

Tomorrow. Arch-Rotarian, he will
Send his cheerful pigs to make
Reconnaissance, investigate
Infernal sprawl, pronounce it fake.

So keep it underneath your hat
If demons seize you by the hair,
For Mainz prefers its porkers fat
And heavenly fodder's everywhere.

II   *Look here, Vladimir ...*

You! European you, with the
Pained fastidious bones,
Take off your exclusive cross and hush
Your cheery omniscient groans.
What makes you suppose yourself to
Be so final an authority
On the stink of suffering's rose?

Do I have to wave an Auschwitz stump
To attest my fitness, *pour
Mieux comprendre* the
Pacific equine rump
Of Bosch, the wart
On the conjurer's nose?

III   *Plus Ça Change ...*

Old Henry commiserates with Hedda,
(A rusted pistol rattles to the floor)
Manipulates as *beautifully* as ever
Seraphic permit to terrestrial door.
Both find that they have in them to agree
Upon the source of their infirmity.

The screw turns aimlessly into the silt,
Hélas, it only pricks a barren spring;
The coupled squeak with boredom from the quilt
Mechanically doing their own thing.
Observing simple pleasures never cloy,
Our pair retrieve their winding sheets with joy.

Totem and Taboo

I

Great grandpa Saqui set in sepia, *The Jew is constrained to flee*
Wall-eyed pensive from a century's nap, *the commotions of Ireland.*
Lingers on an ancient book.
His blasted eyes brook dreaded distance,
Navigate between the darkened Liffey
And the clouded Melbourne stream,
My stem and tap-root trapped in pewter.
Mad Jew-Christ in a tipsy brougham
Rending O'Connell Street with exiled cries
Waving a long onyx at Torquemada's
Hibernian guard and I will go,
He said (mad he was, I repeat),
Go, and let you get on with
Your dirty business.
                        En route he belted *Making course for the tropical*
Mendelssohn's spring song at Victoria *Latitude of the Great Pacific,*
In her glass house, bowed and hurled himself *the Jew playeth upon the organ*
(Satrap second-class) headlong at her *for Victoria Regina.*
Far-flung province, fortified with lemons
For the old sow held his mate in nets too
Taut for even his manic importunings;
And in the turquoise furrows drowned
The northern stars in furious tears.

II

    Claimant to Valhalla's ranks, he took   *The Jew purchaseth a horse in*
    To horse, a bellicose black jewel to   *expectation of salvation.*
    Fly around the Saxon emerald fields,
    Baring his teeth to mock the cocky
    Bastard accent that had dared
    To call him 'Worrier'. And hanging
    At his beck and kick a beggar-king
    On fiery stilts, Jew among Cossacks,
    Bounding quisling to the prayerworn ghetto;
    A pair of violent uncouth coat tails
    Hot upon a nag's behind that arched
    Its banner in his face and plopped the
    Crumbling apples of contempt
    Before his feet.

    Careless of his masters, sparking off   *'Warrior' winneth the Melbourne*
    A thousand fires the thundering jewel   *Cup, 1869.*
    Panicked some seagulls with a windy rush
    And smote apologetic aeons on the nose,
    Unsettling the wavering fringes of
    An aged shawl.
                      If small recrimination   *The Jew findeth not salvation;*
    Ever snubbed the edge of his recruitment   *the penance of life falleth upon*
    Nothing ever found a way to the old sow,   *him.*
    Glutted with her farrow (save a line
    In graceful and bizarrely cautious
    Arabesques of veined ink).

The Chosen—Kalgoorlie, 1894

I   The Escape

His father said: Marry her. She's had a hard life—
With you lighter it can't get. She cooks,
Breathes, a little ankle, eyes not bad ... what
More do you want? For mother's sake ...
Her heart won't beat for ever ... a grandchild, a family!
And he ran away. He ran and ran from that
Abrasive calico breast, virgin ankle, awkward
Menial hands, his heart burdened with crimson sunsets.
(Grandmother-mother, hands that moulded love in me but
Passive lay in his impatient palms). Thin spectacled,
Sixteen he fled the fatherland across the Nullarbor.
His mother had her heart-attack and Yahweh,
Rhadamanthine Yahweh (blest be He!) galloped
Snorting after the little puffer. Bobtails blinked,
Smiling among grey stones to see
God go off His Head.

II   Retribution Plotted

And Yahweh the Extravagant,
Prodigal Yahweh swore revenge,
Stamped in a desert way off His patch:
A Desert-Dweller all My life!
Don't they know of Me? The trumpet-tones
Shatter on flat stones; ant-hills heave,
Turn over in a dreamless sleep:
My Chosen do not stray far! My ways are wondrous,
Perilous; I am the One (no other shalt thou have)
Who does the choosing here!
Braying maniac brewing cataclysms.
Antediluvian mouths yawn
Under the unshriven sun.

III   The Plague

They handed him a key:
This is your house. A sagging box,
Smoke-licked pane webbed by
Sleepy crab-spiders. He'd read
In the old country, Talmud-ridden
Fly, 'In hot climates Spiders
Are able to produce a certain amount of
Local pain.' His skin bristled with small
Spiked crowns. Pain's antidote in peeled
Tub—a pink geranium, stationmaster's ward,
Barren season's suckling.
Weekly his charge gnawed the track to the
Flat horizon, covered a hemisphere in his
Kindled sight, gabbling caterpillar.
But came the Day of the Scorpion.
Clanking, thundering scales, buckling linkages,
From its final poisoned segment issued Yahweh,
Mighty polyphemal ruby eye to sear the spider,
Flower and stripling stationmaster, belching
Plague through flaring nostrils, scattering
Dybbuks through the land.
I CHOOSE, HEIR TO ASHES! Squeaking demons,
Metal-winged, buzz and swoop, pegged within
The confines of His breath.
Ten days he lay reflected in his death, his
Bowels curled limp beside his shoes.
Next train his grieving father
Brought him home.

IV   Retribution Achieved

She said: This is the station key.
Your grandfather watched trains as a young man.
I waited.

Forbearance—Coolgardie, 1898

He soon shall find Forbearance no acquittance

Aunt Phoebe spent her
Rocky middle years inside
A tent upon the goldfields,
Swore at tardy camel trains
And waterless, she rued the day
Of comfort's banishment.

Uncle Barney entertained the
Boys inside their tricorne—
Leathern Bacchus and his pards—
Together clashed the tin pan cymbals,
All agape they loafed around her, shrill
Fermenters of the messianic grape.

Aunt Phoebe gave short shrift to
Her messiah, bore her child and
Fanned her fire and wished
The day would come when hell
Should loose some extra flames
And sear the lot of 'em.

Meanwhile she irritably tried
To rear a plot of green outside
Her pitch, forgetful of her wish.
'Twas granted. The infernal powers
Revealed with one swift scorching puff
That grass roots seldom burrow deep enough.

Don Juan at the Record Bar

Glass-pure drops of sound hang
Fresh in the morning air.
Mozart and his death come
Face to face in the
Saturday supermarket.
                          Put a
Requiem under your own roof!
You idly twirl the stand,
Finger speculates on sideburn
Styled by Mr Troy.
                          Will you
Have it in mono? Stereo? Whatever
You decide we guarantee its
Positively final efficacy.
Look sideways at her long blue-frosted
Eye, alien frieze of narcissistic lust;
Come, you'll play with me, sir?
You strain, and drown. Your
Minted heads discuss the tone: you
Don't have this on stereo? Shame.
Amadeus rolls his chambermaid in
Bed of flame.
                       Braced,
The Commendatore waits behind the door.

Chicken

Tucked snug behind
Proscenium arch a
Baby's stoned to death:
The watchers sit in trembling furs,
Slumped with relief.
Beyond belief!
Come, let's get out before
The peak hour traffic snarls
The bridge. I've got cold chicken
In the fridge for supper—at least
I think I have. Those kids *will*
Gorge themselves. Oh go on,
You can pass! The light's already
Amber, hurry up! I'm dying for a
Cup of tea. Don't talk like that
To me, of all people!
Let's not quarrel, things are
Going so well: Ian's done his maths
And Nigel's sure to top his year.
You've worked so hard with
Him … what's that? I
Had to keep her home. You
Know that stomach thing she gets.
She'll be all right tomorrow.
Well, the wings have had it but
The breast's still there. Or
Part of it. You must be starving!
Can't see why we push ourselves to
Plays like that although I feel
The writer has a point to make.
Some cake? Oh damn, I
Gave it to that child next door;
I'm sure her mother doesn't
Feed her properly. What's the
Matter? Aren't you feeling well?
It'll pass. There's Dexsal in the

Cupboard and a glass is
Right in front of you.
All right, I'll come up later—
What a mess they leave the
Place! Did you say she was crying?
Probably a dream. It's just a phase
She's going through. I'll go to her.
You go to bed. I can't think
What's the matter with my head.
                        There, there, the
Way you cry you'd think I was an
Awful sight. Now be a good girl,
Go to sleep. Good night.

Scoop

Colombian vines, the jungle swirl of
First dank life have lapped his exile;
An Indian wife, a patch of corn and herbs
Beneath a fall of perpendicular gneiss.
The travellers stand amazed above the
Precipice, scan his scars, skin, seek to
Nail his public possibilities, prints of an
Old and private life blur beneath their
Lenses, scrupulous distinctions of revenge.

Hauptmann?
Ehrmann?
Bormann?
Hartmann?

Drum and flute repine among the swelling roots,
The stalking vines have leapt to cover
An old man confounded with detail, at one
With thieves and murderers of
Other places, other times.

A Midwestern Wife

After the funeral came the sons to paint
The house for her, but when the painting
Was half done they quit, leaving a twilit zone
For the remainder of her days.
                        Widowed Lady of the
Moose, ex-Illinois Porkette, her Dewey dead at 45,
Farmed hogs, beans in Tuscola till they came shooting
Out of their ears, Veteran of World War I, Barracks 890,
Built a concrete basement, installed an oil furnace,
Left: a wife
        two sons, Elmer and Willard; one, Jim, died before he counted
        two daughters, Mrs Kathy Bormann and Mrs Holly Grabb, both
        of Mahomet, on the day Amy Schlorff's pet ostrich Herkimer
        ran amuck and outran in fact every man and boy in town. And
Also left:
        five grandchildren
        two sisters
        and a brother, Sonny, who preceded him in
        death, former gardener, groundskeeper and
        nurseryman at Appalachian Bible Institute, Tenn.
        and up to no good most times.
The widow taught school 40 years (junior English),
Was a charter member of the Tuscola 1st Baptist Church
Was a member of Sigma Iota Xi
Was a member of the National League of American Penwomen
And in addition was the author of *Homespun*, a book of
Poems, *Daily Lesson Plans in English*, and *The Cross of the
Redemption*. An exemplary life, season to season, said the
Pythian sisterhood knotting their tails. Smarter than old
Dewey at the best of times, scrambling boy.
That kind don't wear so well.
                        Guarded by successions of
Cantankerous dogs, the rats were kept out of the beans.
Weakening once, she wept briefly in the bean rows,
Stiffened, hired a large and surly boy to rake and
Mow on Saturdays. Death took friends, relations

One by one, perching on her window ledge waited
With blank tact.
      The parched flanks flaked in
Summer storms, dust whirled her round corners,
Spring ice seared the magenta-tipped magnolia,
Charred the fever-bright forsythia, slew her tulips.
Violets kindled like weeds. She tore them up, the
Threadlike rich survival too facile for a driven
Life, began to mumble a little, forget a little, shake
As her house shook uncontrollably in the cunning
Prairie winds that tracked her to her door.
Neighbouring children stole pears from her tree.
The hard old hand crumbled in the summer haze.
     And one day she saw that
Everything was grey, a day no different from any
Other day but she saw:
      Her house was grey
      The trees were grey
      Her hair, the words of her sons,
      Her daughters, all her grandchildren
      All were grey
      Streets, cars, shoes, coats, hats,
      Hogs, horses, cows, goats, squirrels,
      Rats, pigeons, doves, cats and all the dogs
      Were grey and above all the sky was wide
      Grey from the moment you opened your eyes
      And why did I never see it before,
      Why and what does it mean?
Nobody answered.
She didn't much expect an answer, certainly
Not from her grandson Larry potting begonias in the
Back yard, no religion to speak of but not a bad boy,
Not bad at all ...
     She moved to dark and shady places,
Lily-of-the-valley sprang unwanted, past her quince
Blossom, hulking crabapple, and the wild blue phlox.
In the dark waxen leaves rummaged sightless, deaf,
Dumb now, pulling at the toughened lily roots, tearing,

Scattering the threaded waste over the ashen mulch, the
Grey soil of her life. There is no more to be done, and
Took the last bit in her stride.
                              There was no visitation by request.
Donations could be sent to the Blind and the Daughters of
Pythias huddled their crocodile tails against wailing
Prairie winds telling what a shame when she still had
So much go left in her but that's life and
When do we meet again?

Memorial Day & Tornado

Half a planet over they roar to Indianapolis
Flash-flooding cockpits of paternal memory.
Easy-on easy-off gum based shuffle kids trailing
Broad-bellied dust funnels off Interstate 74,
Exploding kegs and cans against tomorrow's corn.
All things being equal, momentous issues have lost
Their moment. Old guards sobered, war being done,
Leave well alone.
        Today more distant Furies have declared
Us a disaster area. Irresistible, these coarse seductions
Of the truth, an apocalypse not more passionate than a
Bit of wind and water. We flare and fold in swift turns
Of national concern. The man who comes to read the meter,
Those flattened nasal body counts on Thursdays were steadier
Stuff. Stocks hold in central Illinois. Centennials, awards
For oratory, homemakers of the month keep the keel
Temporarily even.
Fire brigades are there to put out the fires.
The shabby shifts and glitter of desire are blacked
By years of interminable protestant service as
Over Death We Triumph.
        Quietly a semi-trailer rolls the
Nearby cornfield, slow dream-like rollover driver floats
To rest in a sea of Valvoline drums. Panicked by the
Suddenly huge black funnel snaking his screen, how small
He lies. His nightmare turns, slouches to Kansas, shrunken
To daytime size.

Bugle taps thread pot-holed town to town,
Dim beads frost flat silence. Over death triumph the
Graven brotherhood, Knights of Pythias:
                      Ardrey   Aescher
                      Bagby Bobowski
                      Clabaugh Coonz
           Finkbiner Dye Eberspache Fieldbinder
           Fijolek Filipek Finbloom Fleischmann
           Gentilli Hasenauer Hagen Hoffmeister
           Hapke Harness Harnsberger Heimburger
                    Holmblad Lovby
                    Machula Magyar
                    Maartens Meyer
                    Michie Redlich
                    Reifsteck Rich
                    Zepecki Zemlin
                    Zugenbuehl Zyc
From fresh-mown lanes, green as butchers' fern,
Spring little flags exploding, rearing, waving
Bright and dragonish today. As keen as yesterday
Had never been.

4-Lane Divided

With what intemperate sense of waste did they
Abuse the times, unwinding skeins of wind,
Grey streamers flagging their immense wake to
Soar in limbo flat and meaningless as Utah,
Kindly but firmly fenced away from time, days,
Hours of a country they were never easy in.
Moonman and family pierce a cold pane.
                                          Sun,
Luminous plum through mist, draws south the
Compassless armed with an ambiguously-worded
Proclamation of intergalactic trust.

There goes everybody, there goes nobody;
Men in short thunderbolts thud the measureless
Face of loneliness. Assured in motion span a
Continent like any old backyard, volleying
Towards home sense home.
Exile is to arrive.

Fungus Epidemic

Our coming was black in December, slow grey to
Black and back. Darkness followed darkness, night
Night. Smoothed out by shock we were stripped
Down efficiently for the new season, to be shown
To be divided.
                    Wind reared dead life around,
Arranged in quick sharp blasts lines of wintering
Leaves and bone, ragged cot-cases for our inspection.
People keep saying how normal it all is. They have seen
Disease, the day all the elms in Urbana died overnight:
Stretched beside my husband I have been found unfit
For saying what kind of place is this to bring
Children to when what I really mean is I am frightened
By the smell, the corruption of death, the shouting
Tides of my death specifically, an old woman fallen
Out of space, unready.
                    Flooded, I shake in the dark. My hands,
Encrusted with apple-scab, lame the stride of his dream.
I fumble to replace our fallen leaves.
                    Dark still, and May. Seasons crawl.
Cracked crimson flowerheads bow to grass, whole
Yesterday. A tornado watch is out till midnight.
Terraced by fungus the sycamores strike at us.
Their sickness is clean, white, odorless. I am not
Disturbed by it. The circles of forgiveness have
Shrivelled a little with the year's passing.

Urbana, Illinois

The Garden of the F'u Dogs

Like loping indolent kings, the four of us process.
Survivors of a picnic, sausages and punch, the tidy
Swooping rituals of frisbees crimson, blue, and one
Rubber ball astray in a small fortuitous pond.
The earth is steady, the sun warm and shadowless.
Our subjects a little ungovernable—straggled paths,
Slopes of fern and bracken, wary grasshoppers but
Nothing charmed. Clean white birches, planes and
Hickory, a prodigality of grass and leaves that give
The sky no quarter, harbour no phoenix either.
Another family trails politely silent in our wake.
A little bored with nothing to dispense we move,
Reserve our largesse for the Garden of the F'u Dogs.
Taking stock of distance from a central oasis, one
Tall white rotunda flanked by bronze Buddhas in central
Illinois (have they no sense of the incongruous?), our
Step becomes more formal, a pavane of abdicated will.
Gods (of a kind) are here. Down what seems a mile
Or more of green rectangular lawn hemmed by dark pines,
Expansive, claustrophobic both, we keep our distance.
They theirs. The heavy sinews of a coming storm flex,
Baffle the air grown tight around us. We move on,
Guarded by the rigidly spaced altars of the demon dogs,
Governing our little space with ancient glossy haunches,
Dark blue glazed and sated vigilance.

Allerton Park, Illinois

Little League

Daylight saved at seven for three fathers.
Two white, one black, planted thrusting in a
Field of immemorial caps, the snubby shapes
Of sons.
                    Prairie winds drive back the sky
To let them run. Bat-flick. Legs.
Earth shifts beneath them, tremors shake
The world.
                    'Run, Al! For your life, boy!'
The eternal cry. A dog, stirred by ancient
Memory, pees against the new-leafed birch.
Bark slivers, fine as burnt skin, shake in
The wind.
                  Urged by grey-green phantoms, shapes
Of older brothers drawn from Christmas
Phosphorus and flame to cheer, they hit and
Run as innocence drums in another
Shivering season.

Dogwood

Vanished in winter, trackless. Unwithered waits
Her fierce festival. Prowls the brush a season
To rear again a tainted ivory perfection and
Devour the sky.
                      She has a reputation, this stagey
Unwearied predator, catches cue from an
Intimidated modest cast still raw,
Aghast from snows and winds of Canada.
Silence everybody.
Unrolls a deafening bold corrupted breadth
Of petal. On one swift measured beat
Accents her masterful flesh.
Layer upon layer, shadowed space mimics
Each creamed muscular perforation.
The sheenless green unseeing eyes
Acknowledge nothing.
                    Idolatrous packs press to hold
The perfect prey, stripper of infinite promiscuity.
With one ample move eludes the quest, vanishes
Shameless and unwithered.
                      Crenellated images prick out
In fevered paper constellations minds
That know beauty when
They see it.

Leaving Chicago in December

Driven in upon themselves like old men's eyes
They stare from corners. Not at us.
Children ballooning out of doors stamp
Into black rain.
                    Maimed metal struts the grey
Green river ice, chips and stunted floes hold
The wind in swollen poison currents.
Black stars drive silent snow of an iron city.
Chicago, fretted furnace of old Indian night.
                    Tensed, the bus breasts feckless
Blackened drifts. We stare, my children and I,
Through tinted glass at nameless people bound
To our nameless days.
                    Bridling currents of estrangement
Twitch and well between us.

Republican Attorney & Client

Steel-rimmed Chancey Finfrock towers
Above Virgil Liptrap.
                      Squinting at the
Main street giant, Virgil peers, sinks
Into the whale's maw of Chancey's shadow.
                            His piping drone flares,
Dies, as Chancey's friendly teeth clamp shut
A none too promising case.

Waking

My young sister (last egg of all) thought
She safely black enough to mimic ethnic
Affliction, cried Lawd have mercy
Spare mah soul, hallelujahed allover
The house (a musical family) paining
Me, a prickish twelve, no jew nor black
Neither but whiter than Persil.

And the Lord let her caper, smiled on
Childhood dreamtime, me forgave not, bent
Himself double to push pride, ambition,
Rugos inflavit pellem,* flushed my greedy
Pellets down the wind till fit to puzzle
Pieces back, praised Him, woke
Monochromatic, pointed as Kafka.

---

* 'it (the frog) inflated its wrinkled skin'—from Aesop's fable, 'The Frog and the Ox'.

The Prodigy Ages

Creation of pitch,
Perfect capering child with
Your stony heart and your
Decorous ear, buttoned in
Silence, your
Spirit disjunct.

Creature of atrophy,
Rosewood and ivory, fuming
Pique dame doubled over a
Limp pavane, waterproof
Celebrant of
Infant defunct.

Lot's Wife (Take 18)

Put in a word for life
She said.
Life who needs it who's
Making the scene anyway
He said so
Stuff yr. dissonant
Track yr. humdrum unlit
Undubbed wide-screen
Sepia footage and
Pass the salt
He said.
She did.
Passed herself
On a plate
She did.
That's life
She said
She did.

Projection Box

Art? said
The Poet
Let the
Head-on
Intimacy
Of my nerrrrr
....................v
..............o
..........u
........s
........s
..........y
............s
..............t
................e
..................m be
My Impact. Anything
So naked
And o
........v
....e
..r
w
h
e
1
m
..i
....n
......g
Cannot fail
To move

Paperbacks

Snagged between *Fretwork for Beginners* and
1000 Hints for Handymen, the Poetry.
                       Discriminating, idle for a day
I attend the Contents, soothing page—no one
I know, no one my age. Strangers sorted,
Focused by sex, *View of a Pig*—clearly a
Man. *Helen's Rape*—what else but?
Never woman's heroine ('She always had it
Coming to her,' said the aunts of
Menelaus, 'No pride, that's her trouble.')
Requiem for Plantagenet Kings? Who but a
Male would so squirm? Female madness
Assumes more desperate form.
Titles plead literacy: ('I contemplate', 'I count
For something', 'So you think *you* can scan',
'Not for nothing did I read Classics, major
In History' they shout at me.
But *Bedtime Story for my Son, Childless
Woman, The Abortion, Her Kind,* throw me
A minute. As in most affairs of the heart a
Moral smoulders in it.
                       One must confess, despite
Contrary medical evidence (a Johns Hopkins
Psychologist no less) to a difference,
No matter the thousand mature female
Rats caged with the newborn; who needs
A rat? Menstruation, gestation, lactation
Haven't the dash of impregnation, but
Culturally determined? Optional?
                            Poets tell more than most,
Inflate the heart or pulp it.
Men order such things; women just can't help it.
Enough never enough, the whole hog rendered from
Birth to conception to birth. Man diverts with
Nicely weighed perception, unseemly
(Or so women seem to think) mirth.

                              Small wonder that men then
Like women, envy them even, dimly recalling roosting
Long into the night, high in a star-pricked heaven,
Powerless to write.

Maharishi Consolator

Honolulu, 1968

The guru giggles on his pinnacle;
Plumply potted *Monsterae* adore
The throne. Upon the vinyl chairs
Of the Potala creased by
Celebrated students of the
Truth, a hush
Descends.
God has arrived at the
Appropriate hour.
The arms of Shiva Nataraja flail
The sticky air; east in wary
Truce with west shows lively teeth:
'We are, have always been, a
Spiritual people ...'
The shrine approves the thought.
Respectful whispers glide between
The crenellated plastic floribunda:
'And so it is repeated in the
Fourth Brahmana a lonely person
Has desire of comfort ...'
Epauletted bell-hop hands the deity
A winking glass of frosted pineapple:
'Like you, we thirst ...'
Sly frangipani dances at his
Ear, the point is fondled, held
Aloft ... 'who is indifferent to honour
And dishonour, to whom things sweet and
Things not sweet are equal, then is
He said to supervene the Moods; fivefold
Is this man, fivefold all this
Whatsoever. It is, indubitably,
So. You must believe; I bring
This message from Tibetan peaks.' An
Elevator hums its way to earth, the

Waiter's eye flicks round—jeez,
What a bunch of freaks ... 'Now
Do you have some questions
For me? After life you said
Kind gentleman?' The master makes
A non-commital *moue* and shakes his
Head: 'Truly the Person is
Imperishable. Let man breathe up
And let him downward breathe that
Evil death may not attain
To him. And I say thus, and only
So shall he obtain a oneness, union
With his god ...'
                              Hey,
Calm down, lady. Get him *outa* here!
Enough's enough; our staff is only
Trained to handle perishable
Stuff.

Charity Ball

The demon drink conducts a
Blitz, the classes merge,
A waiter's eye flicks round—
The scions surge towards a
Waitress who retreats and packs
Herself against the festive meats.

Stamping their whiskied image on the
Joint, starched to the gills they
Itch, laced inside black shells;
Thrusting claws tighten a raffish grip
On ocean bed awash with crème de
Menthe and gin, they slip

Towards the evening's end, everybody's
Enemy, everybody's friend. Lift glass penultimate
To national service, old school ties, to widows
Spry in lavender. Pickled with glaucous zest
Concede of all the shows sweet charity
Puts on the best.

Campus Fable

'Seek Wisdom' sang
The fulsome swan
And floated to an
Easeful death. The
Cognoscenti took him
At his word and
Sought.

Meanwhile the bird,
Holed up at Lethe's
Wharf, had changed
His tune, enlightened
By his splendid final
Breath:

'A pity. If I
Had known what wisdom
Comes with dying, I
Might have spared them
Centuries of
Trying.'

His poignant revelation
Passed unheard, and
Seeking still
They waned,
Conned by a
Bird.

Tea Room

Terra Australis, great dumb blonde
And vegetable whore, why did you let
Those righteous AS. bastards roll
All over your fruits? Better the
Wrought-iron Spaniard or
Black Portugee than all the
Civil trousered builders
Of society.

Had those lonely lazy hips
Plumped for swarthier memorials,
We might not now be hemmed with
Tea and eyebrows, wary aqueducts
Alerted to Rome's foe, the slack
Unpolitic admission of two somewhat
Mediocre tutorials.

Literary Board

No one I know. No one my age.
The room—well, looms. On stage
Sit poets and historians, here
Today on behalf of and will be,
Maybe not. Don't ask lest it be
Granted. Kingdoms come and come
Again, dispatch their cultural
Emissaries in hair and snappy
Ties. Black brisk briefcases
Contain what must be contained:
The state of the state of our
Imaginative life, need for new
Forms (vital, meaningful) to
Nail apocalypses on the western
Front. All's still, the room too
Hot and science has once more
Failed: fans don't work, doubts
Are expressed for the future of
Poetry, concern for the ailing
Novel without a thorough knowledge
Of aerodynamics but if anyone
Really wants to he's welcome
To try that switch—

KADDISH

Kaddish

For my Father
born 1903, died at sea, 1967

Lord of the divided, heal!

Father, old ocean's skull making storm calm and the waves to sleep,
Visits his first-born, humming in dreams, hiding the pearls that were
Behind *Argus*, defunct Melbourne rag. The wireless shouts declarations of

War. 'Father,' says the first-born first time around (and nine years dead),
Weeping incurable for all his hidden skills. His country's Medical Journal
Laid him out amid Sigmoid Volvulus, Light on Gastric Problems, Health Services

For Young Children Yesterday Today and Tomorrow which is now and now and now and
Never spoke his name which is Father a war having happened between her birth, his
Death: Yisborach, v'yistabach, v'yispoar, v'yisroman, v'yisnaseh—Hitler is

Dead. The Japanese are different. Let us talk of now. The war is ended.
Strangers found you first. Bearing love back, your first-born bears their praise
Into the sun-filled room, hospitals you tended, city roofs and yards, ethereal rumours.

Gray's Inn Road, Golden Square, St George's, Birmingham, Vienna's General, the
Ancient Alfred in Commercial Road where, tearing paper in controlled strips, your
First-born waited restless and autistic, shredding life, lives, ours. 'Have to

See a patient. Wait for me,' healing knife ready as the first-born, girt to kill,
Waited, echoes of letters from Darwin, Borneo, Moratai, Brunei ('We thought him

Dead but the little Jap sat up with gun in hand and took a shot at us',) the heat

A pressing fist, swamps, insect life ('A wonderful war' said his wife who also
Waited) but wait for me wait understand O wait between the lines unread.
Your first-born did not. Tested instead the knife's weight.

★   ★   ★

Let in the strangers first: 'Apart from his high degree of medical skill he
Possessed warmth' (enough to make broken grass live? rock burst into flower?
Then why was your first-born cold?) But listen again: 'It was impossible for

Him to be rude, rough, abrupt.' Shy virgin bearing gifts to the proud first and
Only born wife, black virgin mother. Night must have come terrible to such a
Kingdom. All lampless creatures sighing in their beds, stones wailing as the

Mated flew apart in sorrow. Near, apart, fluttered, fell apart as feathered
Hopes trembled to earth shaken from the boughs of heaven. By day the heart
Was silent, shook in its box of bone, alone fathered three black dancing imps,

The wicked, the wise and the simple to jump in the house that Jack built: This
Is the priest all shaven and shorn who married the man all tattered and torn
Who kissed the maiden all forlorn who slaughtered the ox who drank the water

Who put out the fire who burnt the staff who smote the dog who bit the cat who
Ate the kid my father bought from the angel of death: 'Never heard to complain,
Response to inquiry about his health invariably brought a retort causing laughter.'

Laughter in the shadow of the fountain, laughter in the dying fire, laughter
Shaking in the box of bone, laughter fastened in the silent night, laughter
While the children danced from room to room in the empty air.

What ailed the sea that it fled? What ailed the mountains, the romping lambs
Bought with blood? Tremble, earth, before the Lord of the Crow and the Dove
Who turned flint into fountain, created the fruit of the vine devoured by the

Fox who bit the dog that worried the cat that killed the rat that ate up Jack
Who built the house: Yisgaddal v'yiskaddash sh'meh rabbo—miracle of seed,
Mystery of rain, the ripening sun and the failing flesh, courses of stars,

Stress from Sinai:

                        Let (roared God)

                Great big Babylon
                Be eaten up by Persia

        Be eaten up by Greece
        Be eaten up by Rome
        Be eaten up by Ottoman
        Be eaten up by Edom
        Be eaten by Australia
        Where Jack's house shook.

            Be (said Jack's Dad)

        Submissive to an elder
        Courteous to the young
        Receive all men with
        Cheerfulness and
        Hold your tongue.

Strangers, remember Jack who did as he was told.

            ★   ★   ★

To the goddess the blood of all creatures is due for she gave it,
Temple and slaughterhouse, maker of curses like worm-eaten peas:

As the thunder vanishes, so shall the woman drive them away
As wax melts before flame, so let the ungodly perish before her:

She is mother of thunder, mother of trees, mother of lakes,
Secret springs, gate to the underworld, vessel of darkness,

Bearer, transformer, dark nourisher, shelterer, container of
Living and dead, coffin of Osiris, dark-egg devourer, engenderer,

Nurturer, nurse of the world, many-armed goddess girdled by cobras,
Flame-spewer, tiger-tongued queen of the dead and the violent dancers.

Mother of songs, dancer of granite, giver of stone—
Let his wife speak:

'Honour thy father and thy mother'
So have I done and done and done—no marriage shall ever

Consume the black maidenhead—my parents are heaven
Bound. I shall rejoin them;

Bodies of men shall rejoin severed souls
At the ultimate blast of invisible grace.

Below, I burn,
Naomi of the long brown hair, skull in a Juliet cap.

Do the dead rot? Then rot as I rot as they rot.
'Honour thy Father' sing Armistice bells, *espressivo*.

The stumbling fingers are groping
To pitch of perfection.

I am that pitch
I am that perfection.

Papa's a civilian again, mother is coiled in a corset,
Dispenses perfection with:

Castor oil
Tapestry
Tablecloths (white)
Rectal thermometers
Czerny and prunes
Sonatinas of Hummel
The white meat of chicken
The white meat of fish
The maids and the lost silver.

Lord, I am good for nothing, shall never know want.

Blinded, I burn, am led not into temptation.

The home is the centre of power.
                         There I reign
Childless. Three daughters, all whores, all—

Should be devoured by the fires of Gehenna
Should be dissolved in the womb that bore them
Should wander the wastelands forever.

Instead, they dance.

Whole towns condemn me. Flames from the roofs
Form my father's fiery image. He waves, laughs,

Cools his head among stars, leaves me shorn,
Without sons, unsanctified, biting on

Bread of affliction. Naked, I burn,
Orphaned again in a war.

The world is a different oyster:
Mine.

His defection will not be forgotten.

★   ★   ★

Blessed be He whose law speaks of the three different characters of children whom we are to instruct on this occasion:

What says the wicked one?

'What do you all mean by this?'
This thou shalt ask not, and thou hast transgressed, using you and excluding thyself.

Thou shalt not exclude thyself from:

The collective body of the family
The collective body of the race
The collective body of the nation

Therefore repeat after me:

'This is done because of what the Eternal did
For me when I came forth from Egypt.'

The wicked wants always the last word (for all the good
It does): 'Had I been there, I would still not be worth

My redemption.' Nothing more may be eaten, a beating will
Take place in the laundry. Naked.

'Honour thy father and thy mother'

What says the wise one?

'The testimonies, statutes, the judgments delivered by God
I accept.'

Nonetheless, though thou are wise,
After the paschal offering there shall be no dessert.

'Honour thy father and thy mother'

What says the simple one?

Asks merely: 'What is this?'
Is told: 'With might of hand

Did our God bring us forth out of Egypt
From the mansion of bondage.'

Any more questions? Ask away and be damned.

'Honour thy father and thy mother'

*   *   *

Yisborach, v'yistabach, v'yispoar, v'yisroman, v'yisnaseh, v'yishaddor,
v'yisalleh, v'yishallol, sh'meh d'kudsho, b'rich hu

Praise death who is our God
Live for death who is our God
Die for death who is our God
Blessed be your failure which is our God

Oseh shalom bim'romov, hu yaaseh sholom, olenu v'al kol yisroel, v'imru Omen.

*   *   *

And he who was never born and cannot inquire shall say:

There is a time to speak
and a time to be silent
There is a time to forgive
and a time in which to be
Forgiven.
After forgiveness,

Silence.

Cleft

One night she headless gave away the
old world, dreamed anew. Men tall and
small and pretty thin slid in
and out of her like
maddened trombones, blasting
her scales. The emptied armour
lay wherein she trusted, tranced,

The hollow vizor's chamber breathed
its last guffaw before
matters got really serious
even at a pinch you might say out of
hand at which nice point the
severed head, wide-eyed with loss
danced towards her orchestrated

Trunk, ready (as ever) with a few
home academic truths: 'Deluded and
unconscious woman! Enact your matey
operations, revisit life, visit the
dead, forage the skull, the skin
the skin,' it moaned, 'but shot you
are of my sublimity.' The groaning

trombones strained in *Liebestod* and,
thickening on her tongue, the dream
did in the dawn.

Dreams

Sleeping badly, he'd wake in a rage
to recover the loss. Loss of what?
He could never be sure. At his age
(hardly love but a spasm perhaps?)

A tight squeeze of the heart—nothing more
he'd assure himself, breathing alone in the
darkness. Yet why did he look to the door
as if something had come and was gone?

Mysterious injury, ill and yet never quite
ill enough, it would seem (for a time)
as if she'd never been. By the light
of a day he'd see a girl walking away

In the rain—a casual profile, the turn
of a wrist, the drop of a head. She
didn't exist, had never. He'd learn
to forget, to begin to forget

He would sleep again. Obscurely and peacefully dead
to the world, breathing easy. Yet suddenly dreaming,
awake to himself in the dark of the bed, somewhere
in an endless passage started to howl.

The Artist

(after Isaac Bashevis Singer)

She spoke the word 'artist'
as seriously as a pious Jew
names God. Naive?

You bet, and tall
with it—a brown-eyed
40'ish female of a kind

they don't make nowadays.
Not, I believe, a barbarian
but almost, I was after

a couple of stories: 'I
guess you'd call me one,'
I muttered, taking notes.

She took all poetry seriously
which goes to show she
wasn't on the uptake. I

set myself to shock her,
a full bottle on brothels
and the confession of sins.

I had material for years to
serve her with, defamed all
poets from old Shelley on

and told her I was fucking
five (women, that is) at the
same time, the words as near

the gutter as I could. To
comfort me for being so misguided
she delivered books and cake

and finally herself: 'You
are so gifted, so deluded
why sink you so in darkness?'

(such flowery phrases came to
her quite naturally), and I a
chronic liar laughed, told

truths however brutal, watched
her eyes take fire from
life's injustice to the

gifted of this world. And
still alive, she'd answer
as if I were hardly there at all:

'You are an artist.
God will forgive you
for your talent.'

Identity

'Our greatest joys to mark an outline truly
And know the piece of earth on which we stand.'
So you may say, and I in part accept the newly
Taken exploration of a whispering land,

But voices in the country of the mind
Tame the crueller aspect of my days.
Irresolute as fine weather, I am blind
With memories. Nature was never friendly, her ways

Severed me and serious poets should never be severed,
Should lovers be, namers of colours, shapes, plants.
Not urban neurotics from frustrate armchairs levered
To stare through glass at bird-forsaken haunts.

Nature poets are rarely as tranquil or composed
As they sound. Wordsworth fussed around, man
Speaking to God, not men—delight imposed
On distraction. John Clare ate weeds. Cowper ran

Mad from the world's disease. Their city hell
My heaven, their order my darkness. 'One vast mill'
Can compass rival landscapes. So I'll sell
The poet's soul for memory's Eden, whirl

The glass above the ravenous soil split
Wide in veined caverns, shaped by affliction.
Seeded in flame, hatched to withstand, I'll pit
Double-tongued desert winds against my conviction.

After Such Knowledge

Disaster around. She has worked hard
at it. Sneer, sniff, cavil, carp

sunder the muddy dignities but
dignities despite. Lovers, husbands,

children, friends alive, dead or
halfway dead steam off.

Half cracked with hope she
wheels on the ocean bed below

their wake, dull bell tongueless
from a cold tower, snagged in weeds.

In what sweet silence rests the bell unless,
bearing a royal pardon, little ships return?

Reckoning

Whom have We next? (His syntax is
perfect). This one is due for what
there is called joy.
                          I alone know
the span of her schooling.
Who else needs to know?
None but I, the Omnipotent.
Under my hat will I keep it
(vernacular master).
                          Her sullen
green fires will I spring
unburden her airs
allow time to pass
and in My pain's darkness
trample her glass.

Three Songs of Love & Hate

1.   The Stone Dolphin

I have prayed for the end of his breath
(and mine)
to what end?

Anger's words have been hugged
and released.
The language of tyranny had to be
learnt if anything were to be said.

What has been said has been said
is still said after the panting
mouth has been clamped by despair.
But led by the devils
do angels leave too?

True grief is tongueless when the dumb
define love's death.
In a fiercely fathered and unmothered world
words are wrung from the rack.

Bury love's face
Bury love's bones
Bury love's tongue
in a place where the cataract groans,
where water is wedded to stones.

My dolphin, you'll leap in the sun,
Caught sweet, without hate,
Without grief in perpetual summer.
I sang you through gentler seas
than you knew, nor will know never.
Time full and perfect made heaven to
laugh in its mercy, made flower the apple,
showered me with innocent petals,
shook birds and fish in the lightning
tides where wind and water merge, melt,
melt and forever melt.

Drowned in the boon of his breath
I gave thanks for his dolphin pride,
for the creatures of water and air
keeping our pace.
Even the airs of the oncoming night
couldn't chill our far fathoming.

Warned, yet unwarned, beguiled by far
kinder griefs, swimming alone and
drowning, I embraced in one
shining sun track a dolphin of stone.

2. Jack Frost

To sit upon her belly warm
Jack Frost has come.
His cold sweet weight
Does not alarm the night
Or shake belief.

Too cold to ache
She parts her leaves
And welcomes thrust of snow
And stretches fingers past all pain
To stroke the teasing foe.

The cold creeps on
The buds unfold and burn
Her into night. Traversed
She lies and powerless to
Thaw the subtle guest.

3. **Tiger Heart**

The tiger heart (if heart it is)
Kneels down within its cage
It laps the famished air
It asks for nothing more.

Orpheus sings alone to master
Nature, stills its rage.
The smallest bird abashed, is
Warmed, the fish fly water,
Spring to him, the wind and sea
Are mute. The trees and stones
March steadily, the river flowing
Upward to the dulcet chant
Springs golden shrimp, anemone.
The lamb and wolf are teased
by hope, they look upon the face
of love appeased, but all's not sure—

The tiger stoops within its cage
And keeps its starving course along.
It will not hear the song.

Lamb

The people press.
They gaze and call it 'star'.
To me it's time for home.
The winking silver points mean
'Stars'—there are so many.
They mean
My master's loving clasp
My mother's tit
And sleep. Then all is black
Till morning.

This is its mother too.
A straw hangs on her lip
And all the folk are sighing for
The little creature as they
Sighed when I dropped bloody
From my mother's hole.
I didn't know then why
They sighed but am beginning.
Cold winds and snows,
The black of night,
Force all of us to kneel.

Ark Voices

Mrs Noah Speaks

Lord, the cleaning's nothing.
What's a pen or two?
Even if the tapir's urine
Takes the paint clean off
There's nothing easier.

But sir, the care!

I used to dream perpetually
About a boat I had to push
(yes, *push*) through a stony town
without water
There was no river and no sea and yet
I pushed a boat against a tide.
It wouldn't float although I pulled and
hauled, my flesh eddying,
drifting with the strain of it.
Is *this* a dream?
Fibre my blood, sir.

The speckled pigeon and the tawny owl
swoop by. They coax me to the edge.

To save to save merely—no matter
what or whom—to save.

Sweep and push of waves against the sides.
Our raft is delicate and our fire
turns wood to ashes.

He takes it well
and Shem and Ham *do* help—you can't expect
too much of anyone can you and
Japhet's still a kid. Their wives are
young and tremble in the rain
their wits astray.
As soon as we're born
we're all astray—at least
You seem to think it's so or else
why this?

I know you promised us a landing but
what a price!
We're dashed from side to side
we strike through spray
the foam blinds Noah till he
cannot steer.
Even the mightiest creature cowers in his
stall panting, snorting in the welter,
bursting prayers upon your path
of righteousness.

Comfort enough I'm not.
To feed and clothe, to bind a scratch I can.

We once moved quiet in our lives
Looked steadily ahead. When I was small
there were no roads across the mountains
no boats or bridges over water.
We farmed, lived simple, circumscribed.
Our birds and beasts delivered their young
in peace. The trees grew tall and now and
then I pocketed a speckled egg, could climb
and peer into the nests of starlings.
Height and blossom.

Then we lived neighbourly with our birds.
Creation, your handiwork, was one.
No good and bad—just men and women.
But with your sages came the rub. We tripped
over our charity. Duty-fettered, love
tumbled like a lightning-stricken tower.

Noah is incorruptible and good, a large
sweet soul.
Sir, I have tried to be!
But does the frog whose home was in a well
assail an ocean?
How does the summer gnat approach the ice?
The flood in which you throne us is to the
universe a puddle in a marsh. Of all the myriad
creatures you have made, man is but one, the
merest tip of hair upon a stallion's rump.

Noah looks into space.
He sees the small as small
The great as great.
He sees, goes fearless at the sight.
I see the small as too little
the great as too much.
Does this diminish me?

He looks back to the past
grieves not over what is distant.
I mourn the wrack, the rock under the
blue sea, our old wound, the
dismantling storm and cannot
thank you. Helpless with what I am
what can I do? This pitted flesh and
madness in my heart, rage at my fear
of you. Am I thus harmless?

Strangers in this ark, this one small 'Yes'
afloat on a vast 'No', your watery negative.

Noah stares impassive through the foam.
I trust in him although our woe, the
trap of my young body, cracked his trust
in me. I bend but do not break under your
chilling stars.

Even the wolves, the tigers must be fed
in these deep-laden waters. Else we are
all drowned bones. Intercede with him
for me, speechless and unspoken to, the
comic keeper of his house.
My sons are fraught with wives, have
waded into deep waters.
A full ship and homeward bound—Yes,
I'm just about to lance the horse's leg.
A large sweet soul and incorruptible
I said. Or have I seen the great as
too much yet again? The speckled pigeon
and the tawny owl have drawn me to the edge.
The drowned folk call to me:
Deliver us from harm!

Deliver, sir, deliver them
and all of us …

Lemur

This powerful tail this tiny brain
Would make of man an ass:

Because of such as me the earth is riven.
Yet I suit your plan and am

Forgiven for it. Lord, you
Surge me clear of pain:

Nor past nor future, duty nor
Regret are mine.

Today today today only
Today I swing upon my ring—

Tailed rung from sleep to sleep to
Hunger   Play   Sleep   to

Leap through blackest night.
A state of grace.

Laved in eternal rhythms
My ailing howls kill time:

We eat and die.

Your eye burns a dark
Angelic arc into my frightened fur.

The rain will wash it clean
Away—before me the flood—

Io Lemuria! Wandering spirit of the dead
Voracious once a year revisit

Those I loved who feed me quick,
Thud wide the door, and shaking pray:

'Manes exite Paterni!'
Leave! Ghosts of our fathers!

Grafted with their pain I go
Only to return

Sir, I fear my part in this haunting

Bat

Born bat-blind
wawled naked
into flight,
parent-pocketed.

          I swerve
from light, see through
my crazy stiffening ears.

Hang-glider of your flood
Sir, I skim
              and
                    whirl
                          dark water.

                      Struts extended,
prop thin skin against your
withering blast.

Whirring within the ark,
claws lurch to clutch at
crevice memories, the hollows
of a feeding dusk.

Come night, and Noah ducks my
fine fur, accurate flap, my
craven pointed face.

My nostrils trail spirals of
shrill screams.

I'm more afraid
did they but know what you
have always known:

by day I hang
like one condemned
to die

Mouse

Though you attend my body, Sir
my high thin cry,
can you bear me in mind?

Before your rim I bob I
whisk and skitter, drill
my mate—O cordial seed-shower!

Humbly born I take your father—
nature on me, eat my young. To
rise again unscathed though

Far fallen. The merest crack in
your creation makes me visible:
small hole in a ripe corn basket.

Docile I fit beneath mine enemy's
foot, sole privacy of death.
Your seas add nothing to my daily

Fear. You prepare me coriander,
caraway, stout barley, lentils,
poppy in presence of my foes,

restrain the green-eyed devil
monstering me, forestall the
leaning elephant, remind the

hamster   weasel   stoat   rat   that

Ashore and in one room
no cockroach can survive
a loose and starving mouse

Mink

In so meek a slink
lies ambush.
    My soft tail
disarms.

Sir, my dreams are violent
even as your waters crash
great trees to earth
like matchsticks.

    Beast that I am
I frolic: why dream beyond this
life so succulent?

My fires leap to the stream's
flow and in a wood I know
whatever moves:
       spring
            scuttle
                 scrabble
                      claw

fury of frisk and gore
and the long strong smell
of a death.

    Close to water merge with
mallard frog heron spiny lobster.
    Whatever moves
is still thereafter.

Immoderate scabrous fisher-king, should I
complain my soul's bitterness? Instead I
eavesdrop on the river's descant
note the soft mottled trout bellies
luminous transparencies of water life.

    I trap,
kill as those made in your image trap me
to wear and warm.

Such silence under fragile leaves
before the spring.

Taken alive my face is known
to wear the devil's cast:

beautiful moon-drinker
sun-swallower

Wolf-Song

Cold blows the wind in the forest,
And quietly drops the snow,
I never had but one lover,
And her grave lies here below
And her grave lies here below.

I'll sing of her death in the forest,
The loveliest of them all,
I'll howl and run in the quiet snow
Till they answer to my call
Till they answer to my call.

They can beat their drum in the thorny brake
They can blow their horn in the town,
My cry shall wake the very dead,
And I shall run them down
And I shall run them down.

Saddled and bridled and booted,
Came three hunters to the vale,
They caroused with the townsfolk merry,
And were told a painful tale
And were told a painful tale.

'There are wolves in our windy forest
There are wolves in our snow-bound plain,
Our sheep and our children are taken
And will ne'er come back again
And will ne'er come back again.

When the moon shines white in the forest,
You can hear them moan and cry,
They hunt by scent in our peaceful vale
And our children all will die
And our children all will die.'

Then up rose the gallant hunters,
They took out gun and knife
They swore they would rid the snow-bound vale
Of the wolves who halted life
Of the wolves who halted life.

They came on horseback at midnight,
They came with knife and gun,
My love and I did howl and cry
And their nimble hounds did run
And their nimble hounds did run.

They came to a break in the forest,
They heard our guiltless cry,
The foremost of the company
Took aim against the sky
Took aim against the sky.

The hounds ran swiftly through the wood
My tender love to take,
And from the very hills and dales
An echo shrill did shake
An echo shrill did shake.

And now there came the panting hounds
And now there came the gun
The foremost levelled it at my love
As helpless we did run
As helpless we did run.

O he has killed my one true love!
O he has killed my dear!
Her blood is springing on the snow,
And I am stiff with fear
And I am stiff with fear.

Whose blood is this in the forest?
What moon shines clear in the sky?
Though I have to wait out seven years
The hunters will surely die
The hunters will surely die.

I've ravaged their sheep by night
I've slaughtered their children by day
O sweet shall I sing to see their blood
Which for that death shall pay
Which for that death shall pay.

The seventh year is upon me
Seven years from her final breath,
I'll howl and run in the silent snow
And lure them to their death
And lure them to their death.

I'll sing of her end in the forest,
The loveliest of them all,
I'll howl and run in the bloody snow
Till they answer to my call
Till they answer to my call.

You can rest, my love, in our forest,
You can sleep in our thorny brake,
For the hunters three today will die
And I their life shall take
And I their life shall take.

O when shall we meet, my dear one?
O when shall we meet again?
When the leaves are fallen from the bough
And the green and the spring are come
And the green and the spring are come.

Tiger

Lord, you know as well as I
who made this fearful symmetry
and why

Truth needs no sign.

Your ark's eaves fret my stride
my pad sinks heavy on this narrow spot
its cubits warp my stalk
hunched for your
sore slaughter.

Beating through unknown currents
veiled cataracts of foam
drench the high hills where
once I preyed.

      Was I not your pride
when first I parted paleolithic fronds to
roll my mate, renew our undefiled
bone and flesh?

Fair as the moon
clear as the sun
terrible as an army with gold-brown banners
on me you set your heart's seal:
son of morning.

Your love was stronger than death.
Your new moons were my delight.
You worshipped the work of your hands.

Howl, gate! Cry, city!
Whelms me the trap of your vast wing.

I'd lief lick up the swollen waters
of your wrath than,
competent to kill, be
smothered in safety:

who would so starved survive?

Hippo Sonnets

He

Weary with toil, my ugly head is large,
My baggy muzzle ponders to the earth,
Against you, sir, I lay my plaintive charge:
That you have sanctioned such misshapen birth
As mine. You call me your creation fair,
Bulbous and rude, I dive into your flood,
Warty and naked, rough beyond repair,
I thirst for beauty. My sluggish substance would
Offend the very bottom of the lake.
I mince upon my well-developed toes.
Snorting violent columns, rise to take
The air with swift extremity. My nose
Seeks out my love timid and perfect, but find
Only my grief, and all my joy behind.

She

Yawning I lingered, drowsy took my ways
Along the high banks, dreaming of my desire:
A single offspring, tenant of my days
To guard and nurture. Shaped in disabling fire
I laboured the monthly courses of the moon,
Met with the loose dull substance of my kind
And suddenly the inventive act was done.
Our wrinkled baby pads along behind
Our ponderous puzzled flesh. He nuzzles warm
Against me. The small bright interim of our love
Blunts my tusks to lift him clear of harm,
Your perfect creation. Sir, if I could prove
The fitness of my longings, would it serve
To know, just for the record, that once I loved?

Giraffe

Front legs spraddled wide
      neck arched
        delicate
         down
          I
      sip O sir
  your rough waters

Within the ark I stifle
paceless, acute spectator,
mustard-and-orange brawn
sky-bather

Why not excess undo and
dock me?
down to size expose me to
feel what others feel, see
what others see.

Taller, more abject I
strip acacia's highest leaves
towards which others strain
fail
fall
short and I long
witness enemies and warn
with soft blunt horn.

To whose advantage?
I'd rather mingle vision
with the ant than, so
removed, command the
lion and the leopard
in my sight.

whirr

I jitter whinnying
kick   bite   bolt
at shadows:
                dappled
forelimb and hindlimb
rock over yellow plains in
blue-hoofed funk. Fly-wisk tail
corkscrews behind: kind winds
favour clownish miles.

Motionless mottle
I blend: am
sun-patches
leaf-clusters
everything
nothing

Whale Psalm

I steer the chastened furrows
with my tail
coil filamented upwards   lift   thrash
down to
crash the
heaving waste
behind.

My captors close
upon me, sir, I call—

                Thew and sinew
peak and plunge: then softly softly
stealthy roll and glide, recoil to
coil again

                lift in subtle curvature
plunge downward:
my ponderous flukes subdue
the darkening flood.

                O sir, you thus
prepared me, thus I churned your path
chanted your praise: my being
spoke your wonder.

                Unmoored from innocence
from your sight cast, today I range
hell's belly.

Earth's nets tighten:
men forsake their mercy, shroud me dumb
who have so loved the habitation of
your waters.

Rein me from darkness now as once
you ransomed Nineveh lest
fishers mourn, nets languish
on the blackening sea.

Elephant

I bulge in my bindings, dream-wrinkled,
dreaming of long slow rivers:
I rend with my pent-up proboscis
your buffeting seas.
                        Pendulous delicate
hybrid of handnostrilnerve; glorious
once could raise rocks, split trunks
pull feathers from air, pluck
nestling from nest.
                        Then rest,
silted in shadow.

Once could paw up jungles in thunder
and trumpets: with one foot wrench
kingdoms asunder, intercept missions
of stars:

war-fossil
power-shard
hack hierophant
temple dancer

now plod mud-slumberous
sluiced in this world's waters
dreaming of long slow rivers
and you, sir
                        the source
                        the source
                        the source

The Poet Gives a Reading

He told them all about himself
and what his parents did to him
and how though lazy
he once showed a slight
but quite exceptional
gift for tinkering
with radios.

How his parents also showed
exceptional patience.
Plenty of expense and trouble
sent him east to study
radio and still more
radio but he couldn't hear
the words
couldn't follow
even the simplest
instruction.

Efforts had been made
Yes,
efforts had been made
to make him normal
O so normal.

He seemed so quick-witted
sane and even
sometimes sensible,
with reasonably earnest
intentions he told them
all about what it was like
to be married to his
wife, what it was like
to be
a father.

He read his favourite
poem about love and walked
up and down up and
down
Then
read another poem not
about his wife but
also about love
or so he said,
and reading walked
up and down
up and down, his thumb
stuck sharp in a brass-
studded belt, buckle winking
as a tow-haired student
asked were poets
real and meaningful
people.

O yes, he said
real enough as
real goes.
A regular western child
I was—
my mother needled my
father cold, my father
drank his pay away and I
stayed young in my
mind as your regular
children do
he said walking up and
down, up and down
his thumb grown
restless in his belt
like the thumbs of
regular children will
when the dragon-shaped
cloud hovers over the hill

and the day turns up
to his wakening look.

A seaman's son with
eyes of blue who walked
up and down like a
stealthy screw
and said about read
about more about love
than your regular
children
do
pinning messages on the
jotting-pad of his mind
to a girl in
white with a dark Indian face
who left after the
second last poem
with a barely
concealed
yawn

The Poet Puts It Away

Keeping his beard on, he moved
into hand-stitched shoes
7-league suits: the buckle's
wink was dim.

            Losing altitude he
entered the 'diviner heaven of prose':
getting closer to himself.
Out of gear
and often in the wrong key,
had haemorrhoids, was ethically in a
mess and, for the umpteenth time, his
daemonic was slipping.

Scholarly research can
excavate the problem from St Paul
till 1980: called psychohistory,
some things are better left alone.

            More subjectively
and not sober, he indicted equally
Dr Heinrich Hoffman (circa 1840) and
his mother (definitely 1907 although
she preferred 1915) for cutting him off
in all directions:

      'The door flew open, in he ran,
      The great, long, red-legg'd scissorman
      Oh! children see! the tailor's come
      And caught out little Suck-a-Thumb'

A close shave either way.
Ever alert for women booze and chocolate
he committed 354 fornications (at least
half were under-age) off his own bat
though he called it 'getting laid':

> 'Mama had scarcely turn'd her back,
> The thumb was in. Alack! Alack!'

Countless airy lies
laid out like glowing rugs for his
imaginative inspection; constant coveting
of his neighbour's ass (he moved house
often); the theft of three books:

> the Gideon Bible from the
> Port Hedland Motor Hotel
> (the word of God ought to
> be free and the Gideons
> whoever they are want you
> to steal it so they can put
> another in its place for
> another lying Priapus to
> simmer down with after
> multiple campus fucks);
> Aristotle's *Nichomachean Ethics*
> (which he assumed nobody would
> ever read and he never got
> around to it either); and
> Henry Miller's *Cosmological Eye*
> (which ought to have proved
> orgasmic but turned out to be
> vaguely mystic and
> put him to sleep. Quickly).

Two cats and a dog met their end by
his motor vehicle, a thousand
winged insects by his hand:

> 'Here is cruel Frederick, see!
> A horrid wicked boy was he'

His father was anything but honoured
his mother positively dishonoured,
hacked up, hidden and easily discovered:

    'Let me see if Frederick can
    Be a little gentleman'

Took God's name in vain daily
put himself inexorably into every
poem without even a decorous
pretence of self-distrust for which
he received high praise.

        Slandered the
Sicilian next door, put away
5000 litres of whisky in
10 years, made his wives
altars of stone and
sacrificed them to
punk rock:

and no (with a sideways look)
today he wasn't friendly either.

Erect in the middle of
thunderings and lightnings
he struck:
        more poems in him
than he'd hoped for but
more than he wished.

        They
had a way of telling
the truth and believing
himself alone in the
storm he heard
none of it.

The Poet Asks Forgiveness

Dead to the world I have failed you
Forgive me, traveller.

Thirsty, I was no fountain
Hungry, I was not bread
Tired, I was no pillow

Forgive my unwritten poems:
the many I have frozen with irony
the many I have trampled with anger
the many I have rejected in self-defence
the many I have ignored in fear

unaware, blind or fearful
I ignored them.
They clamoured everywhere
those unwritten poems.
They sought me out day and night
and I turned them away.

Forgive me the colours
they might have worn
Forgive me their eclipsed faces
They dared not venture from
the unwritten lines.

Under each inert hour of my silence
died a poem, unheeded

ASK ME

I

China Poems 1988

I   Roosters and Earthworms

It's the year of the Dragon.
Omens for the journey aren't encouraging.
No language and I'm booked
on China Airlines. In Hong Kong I dream
that I am born without a tongue
and wake up screaming ...

I'm studying the twelve animal signs.
Or did the Revolution do away with them?
Too frivolous maybe? The Irish in me
thinks there may be something in it
all the same. Keep reading—

Are you a sentimental but crafty Rat?
A dutiful Ox?
A smashing but unpredictable Tiger?
I am a Rooster.
Honest, frank, obliging, difficult
to live with.
Spot on, so far. What's this?
Vain? Despotic? Prickly about criticism?
Perhaps there's nothing in it
after all.

Tradition has it that I'd find
an earthworm in the desert.

My best roles are military hero or clown.
Not much to choose between them but
I'll settle for the latter, never liked
the army much (the Irish rises up again),
my worst is spy—I'm too conspicuous.

Roosters don't mean to hurt your feelings.
They simply like to let you know
your food's inedible, your hygiene's foul,
your creature comforts nil, you're vain,
despotic, prickly about criticism.

Rooster celebrities include:
Catherine the Great, Colette, Copernicus
and Kierkegaard (the company's not improving),
Marie de Medici, Strindberg, Queen Victoria
and, wouldn't you know, Wagner.

I'd better watch myself.
Plenty of other roosters on the farm.
Earthworms never grew on trees.
This is where it all began.

II   Out of This World

I'm in Beijing.
When I was young it was Peking.
Fans and silk and lacquered screens,
sages playing chess in elegant pavilions
on the Flowery Mountain …

It's minus 4.
The heating system thumped all night,
the cistern trickled.
At school we called it Chinese Torture,
gave each other Chinese Burns.
China was a name to conjure with
when we were young, light-years away,
out of this world.

It's 5.30 A.M. and I've been downstairs twice.
Nobody there.

Down in a vast reading room for students
I saw two dogeared journals, *China Reconstructs*,
in a bookcase with glass doors.
Not a book in sight.
Someone left a Chinese newspaper.
I can't read a word. Who am I here?

The water taps are dry.
The colours in my room bring back
Australian holidays, dead brown grainless
pub wardrobes, kitchen-green walls,
dun green felt carpeting.
Under the bed with its embroidered pillowslip
lie two used plastic scuffs. They're also green.
There's a tall red anodised thermos
flanked by two sachets of coarse tea-leaves,
rough as bonsai'd mallee roots. Two mugs with lids.

Something square stands sheathed in black.
Velvet and sinister, it's in a corner.
I lift a flap. A TV set, the antenna's
a Chinese character inside a hoop of steel.
Two diabolic little horns point upward.
Many knobs, a cord, no powerpoint.
I lift the phone.
It buzzes like a thousand swarming bees.
I put it down.

Don't look out the window yet.
Try to deal with what's inside.

At 6 the water starts.
My bath looks like the Red River.
I slumber in the river, part of me
awake on CA Flight 309, marking
before the symptom 'if any now'
Fever   Rash   Cough
Bleeding   Psychosis   Leprosy
Aids
I've got them all.

The river's still,
becalmed above red sediment.

Below the window on a concrete path
a man in black stands motionless.
Black gloves, black coat, a cap.
Is he really standing there
below my bathroom window?
I look hard again holding my breath.
He's there all right.

He's all alone.
The dawn is rising red before him.
He doesn't know or care
that there's a frightened watcher
following his stillness like a dream.

But he's turning slowly now   slowly
like a dream he turns and folds his hands
as if in slowest prayer
first one side and then slowly
to the other, light-years away
and out of this world.

He isn't young.

III   Over the Wall

Today we go to the Wall.
The sun shines, the bus is small.

We loose Australians pile obediently in.
We laugh moderately.
One of us is making a joke.
We can't go overboard here.

Later we'll go over the top
of the Wall. When we get out.

Our two guardians sit up straight
in Mao jackets up the front,
between them a neat pile of paper bags.
Our playlunch.

We're diplomatic and attentive.
I hardly recognise us.

Far down the back sit students.
They are quiet and gentle.
They don't go overboard either.
They may not get out
until the visitors have left.

The sun shines on.
We climb the Wall.
The magic mountains better all our dreams,
their peaks razored against
an endless sky.

Clearly their painters invented nothing.
Looked and recorded
looked and recorded the changeless
whetstoned cones with maybe a man
somewhere down in a corner,
very small and very wise.

We climb and look again.
The eye oscilloscopes along and back
along and back ...

A student carrying my bag is watching me.
She smiles. 'You like it here?'
How can I tell her that
I'm neither happy nor unhappy?

How can I tell her that I've seen
a man at the foot of these ageless peaks
a man who has turned away,
a man who is very small and very wise?

She might think I was seeing things.

IV   Passing

Dreams are the suicides of the well-behaved.

Do the Chinese have great and wonderful powers
of forgetfulness?
Or do they dream like anybody else?

I met a man living in the same building
as the man who killed his father.

He refused to take the lift
in case he met this man.

He walks up six flights of stairs twice a day.
The lift passes up and down slowly
and he watches the iron cage pass.

I dream a poor boy's dream of China,
the story of silence.
The men who pass his father's grave each day,
and walking, raise their caps slowly
without speaking.

Tiananmen Square June 4, 1989

Karl Marx, take your time,
looming over Highgate on your plinth.
Snow's falling on your beard,
exiled, huge, hairy, genderless.
Terminally angry, piss-poor,
stuffed on utopias and cold,
cold as iron.

I'm thinking of your loving wife,
your desperate children and your grandchild
dead behind the barred enclosure of your brain.
Men's ideas the product, not the cause
of history, you said?

The snow has killed the lilacs.
Whose idea?
The air is frozen with theory.

What can the man be doing all day
in that cold place?
What can he be writing?
What can he be reading?
What big eyes you have, mama!
Next year, child, we will eat.

I'm thinking of my middle-class German grandmother
soft as a pigeon, who wept
when Chamberlain declared a war.
Why are you crying, grandma?
It's only the big bad wolf, my dear.
It's only a story.

There's no end to it.
The wolves have come again.
What shall I tell my grandchildren?

No end to the requiems, the burning trains,
the guns, the shouting in the streets,
the outraged stars, the anguished face
of terror under ragged headbands
soaked in death's calligraphy.

Don't turn your back, I'll say.
Look hard.
Move into that frozen swarming screen.
How far can you run with a bullet in your brain?

And forgive, if you can, the safety of a poem
sharpened on a grieving night.

A story has to start somewhere.

The Temple, Somnapura

Choose for your Stone him through whom kings are honoured in their crowns, and through whom physicians heal their sick, for he is near to the fire.
                              Rosarium philosophorum (1550)

I   Ganesh

Footfall
smooth   cool
soothing the sole
arched and released
soundless in
underworld spaces

tread inward
down and
down   slow
slow
lightening the arch
press   swaying on
smoothness on
oiled pilgrimed
soles softened
to yearning
stone
down

Footfall
released arch
loosed to the
edge
the edge
and down
inward
inward—

Faith is the sound
of a man breathing
alone in darkness
emptied

Faith is his patience
tenure on foot-fastened
stone
prayer to an
absence

To learn the Emptiness of the bare mind
Without knowledge ...

Is truth so smooth
so bald
so stark
so dumb as temple stone?

A light shaft strikes the stone,
mints spry slumped corpulent Ganesh,
elephant-crowned runt
of jealous Siva,
the enormous first parent—

Grant, O Lord, we beseech Thee
won't do here—

Affliction fathers gods and men,
our first shame equal.

Ganesh leans his ponderous bulk
upon the open world, his trunk
ripples with laughter.

Pad slow   slow
moulding the foot
to the swell and the fall
the cool stone
breathing—

Echoes swirl the ancient ceiling
voices   voices
cries in little flames lick
sacred texts in smoke
half-caught forms
bells   incense
    dung

Light the tall bronze lamps.
Feed them oil.
Twist the wicks to flicker
over blue-black hair—

Siva's eye beheads his son
and there he sits, docked,
bowed in elephantine sorrow.

Even gods may be ambiguous,
hate their wives,
their children.

His hands fold slyly in prayer,
lips part like shells
to whispering waves of stone—

Women kneel in pious shadows
tracing sinuous whorls of coloured flour,
wisped by incense.
Blue-black oiled hair, white gleaming
cluster upon cluster climb,
trembling jasmine, nightshade, marigolds
garlands of orange   green   gold—

Astride a bandicoot
lord Ganesh laughs.
A short fat marvellous child
bulbous bright, four arms
blistered with bees
three eyes behind his
rippling trunk—

Slumbering in stone
he leans upon the whispers of the dark,
night's nursery.
His fine molested grace remembers
promises of love
towards his difference:

Indra's goad
Padmavati's lotus
coloured inks from Sarasvati
a tiger skin from father Siva
a sacrificial thread from
roaring Brihaspati.
And from the goddess Earth, a rat
to draw his stunting chariot.

Becalmed in stone
his lotus face smiles down
amused and absent—

Retreating from the light
of his now-fathering force,
our human shadows print us small
like crippled children.

II   Vishnu

No precepts here
but slow unravellings—

>   Vish
>   nu
>   Kri
>   shn
>   avish
>   nu
>   Krish
>   na
>   a a a a

pitched against the One
the One forever changeless God
who swaddles mutinous children's hands
and stops their mouth—

The body and the soul know how to play
In that dark world where gods have lost their way.*

Light air and silence kiss
the lazy lotus lip.
Vishnu, rapt in fleshless sleep
under his curly crown,
once tumultuous

The sun, a scorching nectarine
rolls aside the misty scarves
wreathing the violet blur of
distant hills. Green hosts of parakeets
all shriek and blaze and dazzle
divine the coming of the god. Morning quickens,
mounts. All moves and sways suspended.

*   Theodore Roethke, 'The Partner'

Tilting crows cut ever-widening circles high
above the creaking sway of carts
a steady bullock chomp of straw.
Well-wheels grinding   grinding grinding
tiny matchstick forms dot out
the hazy wakening fields,
the long slow hum of breathless morning.

Pensive wives of cowherds toss
on tousled beds.
Come, lord Krishna, hear their song:

>'My pillow won't tell me
>Where he has gone,
>The soft-footed one
>Who passed by, alone.
>
>Who took my heart, whole,
>With a tilt of his eye,
>And with it, my soul,
>And it like to die.'*

Our lord with lotus eyes
has raised a mountain.
Dark as storm his blue-black wings
lift all of us dark stragglers
to glory.
           Spending his force
against soft-bellied rush of musk,
dark turns fair, rain turns fire,
forms dissolve in music.

---

* Theodore Roethke, 'The Apparition'

Balm to fissured earth, he shimmers
to his flute, filling the fervid lips
the thighs that spin like bowls
upon a potter's wheel.
Such tricks and turns take milkmaid,
cowherd, flowergirl, goddess all as one
while tender-stepping herons sit and
strut and rock the limpid waters by
the cunning groves of Vrinavan.

The pleasure lakes brim white with lilies
aloes saffron sandalwood when Krishna,
sleek as an otter, teases his way.
His love drives headlong like a spear
through a green tree.
The pliant women swell and fret and foam
like indolent water weeds on stormy seas.
'Tell us your name' they beg,
trying to recall his face—

Vishnu naps and multiplies.
He has a million million years to go.

Lord of the wheel has shattered shame
in myriad shapes.

He smiles to think how once
a slippery blue-black boy leaped out of swaddling
into sunlight, becoming fish, wild boar, a million
magic shapes ...

Silence flowers on his lips.
The temple garlands wink in candlelight,
their musky clusters soaring to
a solitary half-heard flute.

III   Siva

Though dancing needs a master, I had none
To teach my toes to listen to my tongue.
But what I learned there, dancing all alone,
Was not the joyless motion of a stone.
                    Theodore Roethke, 'The Dance'

    God-step

Upraised palm

    phat!

two subtle fingers
seeking upper air
and up the high-
curved thigh—

Stone stirs to circling music

cobra shoulder snaking
          round
                  and
   down
       the arm flows
     down a
            length to fine-
    point
fingers
        down
  and
     down to
   tapered limb
    to
   rooted
    foot

Eternal joy outleaps the
flame-spoked wheel.

Tongue lags and leaden lies
before the lightning miracle of dance.

Healthy and terrible, Siva sifts his memories
like rolling sesame seeds and dancing, sings
a song of hearty tyranny:

'My voice rolls out in thunder claps
forked the lightning of my weapon's flash,
cuts zigzag paths for my far-seeing,
my tongue a breaking wave.

I grind the earth—it rocks.
I rend the earth—it quakes.
Firm as the earth's axis is
my high-arched foot—

it tumbles the mountain buffalo
pounds burial grounds
topples garden coconuts splits
figs like peas—'

Such childish rages!

Ah, they said, *but children only
curl their lotus toes and stamp unseasoned
lie and sprawl exhausted.*
                         *Siva knows
what secrets curve a foot
the weight   the measure
height and depth of planting.
Let him sing out his season:*

'I land like a vulture on rocks.
My eye sinks sun and moon
the hooded snake my eyelid,
my slinking tiger-shadow lurks, my mount
a gravid elephant.'

New shapes for old! New shapes for old!

'Like dreaming moon in water   or mirage
on the wide spring plain,
nothing is changeless.

Going I stay
Staying I go

My anklets clash I
raise and curve my left haunch
high   higher   higher
     above   the
           rooted
              foot
                      and ever round
    the fiery wheel
        turning   turning
            turning.'

Dusky powdered human forms
flit shadow-black, blue sapphire-
faceted in fitful spurts of
candleflame
Smoking censers swinging golden
chains linking tiny tinkling bells
surging swinging silken saris
jewelpoints sandalwood   sheen of
musk-oiled hair merging into
      light   stone
          silence

IV   Devi

Only Siva, meditating,
could be immovable
in her moving presence.

Tread slow   slower
inward and down
soften the loosened
arch lower
lower   heavily
down
downward to
smooth softened
sole   rising
falling
breathing in
darkness
down—

Ganesha's mother
mother of life
mother of death
sealed in man's
misgivings—

she sanctifies the morning
with her sightless eyes
calm   unhaunted
broad rounded haunches
breasts and melon-swollen
belly, heavy thighs
a massive fruitful
cluster ...

What sways the soul
is what's invisible.

Light breaks bronzed
over these fecund rounds
flexing around the fluid
girlish waist, curving up
and around, so slender
leaflike chaste, mocking
the dense exuberance
below.

Once a girl, a green thing
quickening, she couldn't guess
beyond the clutch of wind
and flame the rising
falling spiral, bud to
fruit to bursting
back to aching blackness
of infirmity to
ashes, compost.

Once a girl, she sang
without a mouth, high
on a granite mountain—

a floating tenderness
brief as twilight
upraised tendril arms
swaying hips and silver
circling anklets rounding
slender legs drawn
down by beauty's
weight to
earth.

Her water pot of bronze
shining in the setting sun
plumbed wells of deep content,
her parents' borderless kingdom.

Days fell silently like leaves.
Words moved slow as glaciers.

But warring gods and demons pushed
to woo night's daughter,
monster-husbands.

Her bowels turned brass and iron
breasts burst with bitter milk
the rocking thighs imparting
shape   pitch   weight to mouth
agape—
her eyes drained sorrow's
salty marshes.

O gentle angry mother,
girl that man knows nothing of,
stretched high on a volcano's rim
voicing the tribe's cruel energies:

        a meditating head from Siva
        arms from Vishnu's vigorous fires
        from Brahma's thighs the passionate feet
        from Indra's serpent shape a gliding waist
        the brush-fire of her hair from Yama
        breasts from the ardent moon
        thighs from forked Varuna, all-enveloping
        god of waters   ears shelled from
        the wind's streaming   teeth   white
        as curd from the nine Prajapatis
        under a sullen twilight brow
        eyes fish-pools deepening
        into oblation.

Ample water jar
bath of birth   vessel of death
      grain-giver

Lady of milky rain
brooks   streams   fountains
indifferent—

Lady of scorpions   serpents
goose   crowned heron   quail
indifferent—

Lady of bull   goat   wolf   deer
hunting and hunted
indifferent—

griffin   phoenix   sphinx
indifferent—

Lady of caves   tombs   skulls
indifferent—

Gods and men have mothers.
We are her infants slumbering
like sleepy planets
circling endless whiteness—

We suck and turn and
hide our faces.

Footfall

sightless   all-seeing
godhead   cobra-smiling

absence

a lotus opens,
suppliant in
sunlight—

Four Poems from America

I   Father in a Mirror

In the morning mirror
you are here in me   my eyes
surprised as from our bitter Sundays
cautious, hopeful
silent.

You said, *If it weren't for the Americans* ...
while I fought on the other side,
a sullen parody of independence
back in '46.

But Dad, you're here and
I'm the parent now, the shy
explorer taking care and looking
for you at you
in America.

II   **Southern Spell**

The Apopka Blue Darters are coming to play
coming to play, coming to play
by Lake Osceola in spring—

Aloisus and Shad
Sylvie and Tad
Nancie and Tabitha and Quinton and Ziggy
Archello, Idalia, Rocco and Lili
Fleetwood, Cecilia, Wink and Clarissa
Dessie and Ulmo, Tibor and Jitter
Zippa, la Donna, Hub, Thane and Rusty
scamper and nibble by Lake Osceola.

The Apopka Blue Darters are coming to play
The town intellectuals have all run away.

It's a great day!

III   Jack Frost in Florida

An unexpected place to take his ease.
Will it appease his slow fatigue?

His eyes ablaze with
Oranges   Oranges
more
a hundred
thousand burning in the tracings
of his hourless breath.

He glides upon them
like a storm
clamping their fires out
one by one

his cloaking dream furls
fouls a green-gold world
to brown to
black to

sleep, Jack, sleep.
World, button your coat tight.
Black is white.

IV   Band Music for a Grandfather

Why should I fear death today?
My daughter is tooting her bass clarinet
in a real American band.

the high school band
the high school band
the neatest band in this jumping land.
She plays with Chuck and Dwight and Wayne
Elvira and Jimmy and Toby and Jane
and O America salves the pain
as the music soars and roars in the rain.

The space shuttle's up and my spirit's away.
O say can you hear your little one play?
Say, should I fear old death today?
O say

A Tale of the Great Smokies*

1   **Otis Makes a Wheel**

> *I have neither the looks nor the*
> *stature of the immortal gods but*
> *am a human being.*

Any kind of hard wood will do, she said
but soon, make it soon.

So I made wheel and hub,
bench and head post of white pine,
spokes of cherry.
The front leg cut from our white poplar
by the well, back legs of maple.

I turned the rounds on a water-lathe,
driven by the stream behind our house,
even with my axe hacked out the dovetail
notch that her thread might
lie easy.

I split the rims from one straight
green white oak and thought my arms
would break. She soothed and urged.
Each day I brought a little of myself
for her approval.

Each end was tapered,
and I drew the split into a circle,
caught the ends together with some pegs.
Then set the wheel up in the attic,
pressed out flat so not to warp it
out of round while curing.

---

*   Italicised epigraphs to each section are taken from E.V. Rieu's translation of Homer's *Odyssey*.

Soon enough, I said, these things
can't hurry.
Like me she'll come to live with limits
Like me she'll learn what can't be taught.

Somewhere beyond all this drift
the stars are reckoning us up.

2   Penelope Spins

and there she wept for Odysseus

Turn from the word
turn away, he said, schooled in silence.
Made a true wheel, then easy
as breathing, moved down the river
poling his skiff into mist.
                                            Thin neck
stiffening, set up to catch the winds of this world
in the long hot shaft of our dying summer.

Loving too much, not enough maybe, hardly a
seeker but cheerful. He had his illusions—
we were one of them.
Things went much as usual.
Maybe the stars had a hand in it,
or the one fixed star of my own
grim seeking whose light
blurs my sight like a
drunkard's candle.

Tread air, tread light
silent as dust riding darkness.
Treadle and turn,
black bobbin fat in my fingers.

Soft as moth's breath,
threads slip through tides of my handling,
wordless to wait on his coming,
fixed in my longing for speech.

Compost   black currant
fodder   horse urine
hickory   smoke
                  Breath lives,
wavers within.
                  Far below, wide
over the valley burn farmlights
through fog. Dusty signals from
neighbouring hearths.

Tread air, tread light
silent as sleepers in darkness
treadle and turn, unlearn
the bulk of our being, unwind
the tight bobbin. Stand
naked as two spindles saying
in one deep-drawn breath
'I am.'

Tread air, tread light
turn again, little wheel.
Darkness has secrets that
light never owns.

3   **Uriah Mack behind the Sassafras**

It's either a goddess or a woman.

She doesn't see me. My pulse is a trout
in my wrist.
                       The hen tails her string
of yellow chicks with alarm to the barn.

She sleeps in herself like a stone
in the sun, shaping the threads
of his going.

She sings to the air, winding,
unwinding the threads:
'Turn again, turn again
little wheel ever.
He shall have what I am
when he crosses the river.'

Neat as a bird in her red headscarf,
loose blond-greying hair
sun-bleached eyes scanning water.
A distaff of ripe dark wood
pressed close, under her arm
near her breast. Puffball of
rusty black fleece near her shoulder,
spinning the old way.
                       Brown fingers plucking
teasing the strands drawn under
to wind the black bobbin as fast
as the wind.

Still centre of everything, sun-worn
like stone, hands leaping
caressing like drunken butterflies
fretting the shuttle.
                              It snags on a
hickory twig at her foot.
Bending to free it, I move.
She backs off, her eyes an unblinking
promise of instant refusal.

There but unseen, suspended to rock
in the wake of her song, I slouch
through the path of her
passionate waiting, scorpion
under a stone.

A daddy's house is nothing
but a cardboard box.

4   Otis Raises Sheep

> *The fruit never fails nor runs*
> *short, winter and summer alike.*

Forty years I tended flocks
on Blue Ridge like my pa before.
We grew the critters just for wool—
a smaller and a hardier strain, no
bigger than your average dog—you
couldn't buy 'em.

Most everybody back
when I was growing up just
kept the ones they wanted.
Stood the cold, the barren times,
never sickened.
Shy and timid too, they ran
in fear from feral beasts,
would let themselves be killed
without a fight. Once caught
and scared, they just gave up.

Most was white but now and then
a black cropped out.
We liked a black born onst
a while. It saved us
from the dyeing.

We shared the extra wool with them
that didn't keep a flock.
Come spring, I fenced the yard and
turned them loose to graze the mountains.
Maybe they'd come back for salt
once a month or so. We didn't take it
to them on account of fearing
that they wouldn't come. You give 'em

salt. Two, three days after they're
gone again.
                    All summer long they'd go
a long ways off and stay.

                  In fall we'd get out,
hunt 'em up and bring 'em down
through winter.

To tell our own, we notched their ears
on top—Uriah Mack, my neighbour
split the whole ear through
to make a swallow-fork.
I knowed it when we swapped a ram
or two to keep from interbreeding.
We had our marks and knew our own,
but shared.
                  Times were the rams would
fight but mostly get along. The
old ones on the mountain had those
long curved horns they'd lock together.
Times were when they'd starve to death
locked in struggle. We found a couple
once, overbit and swallow-fork dusted
with snow, but still we knew the owners.

She wanted to be sure they'd come
down from the mountain in the cold.
I told her often enough they
had to come, just like we do.
                  When they want
a thing or two they come. They
wouldn't hardly if they didn't
find a need.

A home don't need no fences.

If anything gets after them
they know to come.
Like us, they want a place at night
to stay, a barn for heavy snows
fine grasses—blue or tender rye—
blades off cane. And voices.

I tell her every time they all come
back. She's only happy once they're
fastened in the barn and feeding.

5   **Penelope and the Lambs**

> *the gods had robbed them of their parents,*
> *left them orphaned in their home; and yet*
> *they lived ...*

Spring was always best,
took hold of me like nothing else.

The land's slopes softened green
and graceful right down to
the valley, downward rolled
the children, shook themselves
like little dogs in dotted
fields of lavender.
                    Then lambs would
wobble up to suck their ewes
who sniffed and pawed them
into patience.

The old kind nursed their young,
would hold their jug up for 'em,
push the baby to it—either
take it or you die—was in the
tilt.
           No matter what the cold,
they'd clean their babies, dry them
with their mouths, hold breath
right up against them. I'd catch
the puffs of moist warm air hanging
round the little strugglers
in the chill of morning.

There was an orphan once.
I raised it all the way
till it was grown. Then
took it to the barn. It lived.
That beat most things I've
ever seen.

      It followed me all through
the house and if I'd get away, it
just stood bleating like my children
when I left a room.

If a mother died, he'd shut the lamb
up with another ewe and force
the feeding on a stranger.

We saved a lot between us,
thinking over.

Spring was always best. To yawn and
stretch and look and love it all.
Even the dark edge
of the distant wood.

My thoughts like little pine cones
float in warmth like feathers,
puffs of milkweed.

Dogwood's thick white petals
fretsaw clean against the four black cedars
by the well, the tender push of green
by oak and walnut.
It catches at the heart, almost
like a sorrow I might say
if I didn't know it different.

Roses, phlox and pansies cut a fancy apron
round the yellow house, and everywhere
the smell of wood-smoke, dewberries
the river.

Silenced by joy,
the colour, smell and sound
of everything answer
any question I have
ever asked.

Why talk of time, children, spring
and a river if not to tell
that once we spoke and
listened to each other.

6   Uriah is Hired by Otis

> *Who knows but we may oust him*
> *from the threshold and the door ...*

Help her when I'm gone
like neighbours do, he said.
She'll need the shearing
come spring and maybe
early fall.   See that the
well don't dry, the house
stays warm. I ain't been parted
but two days from her before.
I'll pay.

The sun was setting like a big red ball
and yes, I said,
it wouldn't give no trouble
helping out.
There ain't a broken thing
I couldn't fix and
where, I said, my mind
a nest of buzzards, would
you find a dreaming woman
like your own?

I guess a body's like a house
he said, thin and even, but
the spirit keeps on moving.
This time, he said, I'm
putting two and two together.

Seems, I said, like putting
two apart. I don't know
about spirits but this body's
staying put. She won't give me
no trouble. She's smart.

I've watched her spin and weave,
no age on her at all. Most
tenant wives are not the kind
you want around for long, but
yours ... you're more a fool
than what I ever thought.

He went that summer.
I waited out the winter
till she sent her boy to ask
for shearing in the spring.
If he can help me hold 'em down,
I said, it's twenty head a day
or more, taking the measure
of everything. They're small,
remember; nothing much on legs
or tail—it shouldn't take
but six at most.
Maybe, she said. I'll feed you
give you room and pay like
Otis said. Lady, I said, there's
some around that certain things
mean more to them
than money.
                I asked her what she
thought a man was made for.
She never answered. Called the
hen quick into the barn,
her straggle of yellow chicks
behind her.

      'Turn again, turn again
      little wheel ever'

That song again.
Buzzards hatch in spring too.

7   **The Shearing**

> *He'll have your nose and ears off with*
> *his cruel knife, rip away your parts*
> *and give them raw to dogs.*

The boy was watching sullen
as I held the first upright,
front legs stiffened
in my grasp.

Cut sure and deep around the neck
the head and down along the
heaving belly
down to hind legs limply splayed
the soft crotch twitching
peeled the curling sheath
off one side. One fat layer.

Just like you skin an animal,
the boy said rigid, pale,
standing aside.

Then fastening the head
between my legs, I shaved
in one fast sweep the
back of neck and shoulder
smoothly down the back
to tail, then down
the shivering flank
in one swift rush
of fattened fleece.

It's like you skinned
a rabbit or a bear, he said again
or something else you wanted bad.
That kid.

She came to gather up the fleece
for washing, filled a metal
tub, hot water and lye soap
and scrubbed. Then laid it
out in heavy swatches to dry
on clean rocks by the stream.
Never spoke a word, not even
to the kid who stood aside
sullen, pale.

I took another sheep between my legs.
Its muscles bunched against my hands.

You have to give them time.

8   The Dyeing

And now, as easily as a musician
who knows his lyre strings ...

First threads and last.

Smooth thick pale cow-cud
green darkening through oak
past walnut to the pine wood's
distant rim. By now
I know its darkness.

I have dreamed of water.

His flesh was green, the taut
skin of his neck and every
tendon straining out, his face
white against a cold green wall
of water like the stream that
turned his lathe.
It pulled and sucked
swirled mud beneath our feet.

We were suspended so.
Erect in turn, green currents
curling, dimpling round our
naked shoulders in ever-widening
slow dark whorls.

Suddenly I stood against the rush.
It slowed, advanced its tall and
stately waves in a most
sinister silence.
And he was gone.

I didn't know a dream
could be that cold,
its fingers moulding
probing at my bones all day.

The wheel turns.

There's green for birth and spring
in dogwood eye and cedar shoot
and green for death by water.

Unbroken circles loop themselves
tight to the loom's taut warp.
Tension takes time, and
like he used to say, you
can't hurry some things.

Green thread glides from shuttle
feeding from the steady spool.
Weft spins off bobbin
and back in circles
circles …

I washed the plain white wool
in a copper tub. The hired
man started on another ewe,
his mouth like weathered rubber
pursed in silent whistling.

In my tranced discipline
I boiled green oak leaves in a bag
with salt and vinegar for mordant,
strained out the leaves and stems.

A clean unfaltering green.
Wordless.

II

Broadway Vision

And in my dream I saw
a man upon a bus on
Broadway at 100th west.
His jaw pure kangaroo, his
nose both wise and black
and bearing spectacles.

Make haste, O God, deliver me
make haste to help, O Lord

No trousers, underpants with
stripes and limp descending
sox. I prayed to wake as
my straphanging neighbour
pressed against me wise
and black upon the bus.

O hurry, Lord, speed to help
your homesick servant

I sought to move, to leave the
brutish bus. In vain. His way
was forward. He moved speedily
as I backslid. And as he
pressed, I pleaded with the
driver in my uprightness:

O help me, Lord, to pray
for words are slow to come

Obey my voice, was what I
would have said but tongue
was locked, confounded.
No voice came. Instead, grey
desperate vapours spread
from nostrils, ears and mouth.

O clear the air, dear God,
release my tongue

Besides, the driver wasn't
wearing trousers either.
How can man trust a bus's
destination when no girdle
cleaves the driver's loins?
You cannot and I didn't.

O Lord, make haste
deliver me conventionally

When suddenly a storm smoked
up the windows, towering
clouds blocked out the light
and hail and thunder split
the sky. I strove in silence
with my beast from whose—

O Lord, I can't believe
this bit—

sharp pants were coming
tongues of flame! A trumpet
voice waxed loud in Aramaic:
'Stop the bus! She wants to
leave!' accompanied by balalaika
in the right-hand corner.

O Lord, my swift deliverance?
my help?

Alarmed, the other passengers
divided like the sea. With
faces harder than the rocks
beneath they cursed my *sansculotte*
assailant who then sank
upon his evil kneecaps.

For the day of democratic wrath
is come. And who shall withstand
your communal pressure, O Lord?

Behold, I am standing at the door
of the bus, and am set down at
116th west in Broadway, NYC
safe from tribulation and untrousered
men with spectacles and
heads of kangaroo.

O blessed Lord, you heard my prayer.
From such tight spots have you delivered
me often enough amid the difficulties
between birth and death. But how much
longer will your patience hold?

And as I sang the praises of my saviour
I looked about me in the busy street
and lo, there hurried men with jaws
like kangaroos, with noses wise and
black and bearing spectacles. No
trousers. Underpants with stripes.

I thought I was awake. It seems you
favour those asleep, O Lord.

The women all had pouches on their
bellies, some with young and all
did flee apace with joyful din in
NYC. Only I had neither pouch
nor child. My name was blotted out.
Awake, I longed for home.

I am much afflicted, Lord.
Let me truthfully remember
what it was to be at home.
Quicken me kindly out of
silence to speak the danger
of being too much oneself.

The Call

for Charles Causley's 70th birthday

hello Charles how are ya
mate remember William
Creek I can't talk
long there's other fellers
waiting and a string of
camels kneeling on the edge
of nowhere and a bloody
great phone box stuck in
the sand like a dunny with
everyone wanting to use
it no poetry's nothing like
life not mine anyway if what
I think a poem is a poem
poets are born not made just
like you said but life does
help eh tell them all to drop
dead I'm talking to a poet
yes it's Australia saltbush
sand and spinifex and 45°
in the shade last week not
Cornwall in the winter eh
the South Australian manager
of Telecom told us it will
change our lives a facility
he called it for what that's
worth Bernie's cranky it's not
hotter they'll do just about
anything for a dogfight here
gets chilly on the Simpson
three dogs and a road train
full of horses for the knackers
in Whyalla and a bunch of
paper men photographers the
blokes who put it in and

tourists looking zonked the
manager unveiled the bloody
thing usually only six of us not
much to see and less to do
bit of a treat really otherwise
we wouldn't get to see each other
all that often spotted nearly
sixty all in all here today and
gone tomorrow plus the manager
that young stuffed shirt a
trendy wouldn't touch the amber fluid
wanted wine facility this
facility that me camel's got his
nose in piss off you whiffy bastard
not you old mate I'll write a
proper letter later none of
this microwave stuff with
pips to stop congratulations
anyway there's a strangler in
a cowboy suit bashing down the
door and me camel's dropped
his bundle see ya

Pie in the Sky

for Gwen Harwood

I'm eating an Australian meat pie,
reading a book about
Beethoven's spiritual development.

It's very quiet in Hobart over Easter.
They're all in church.
The pubs are closed.
I've struck it lucky at the deli:
he's Greek.
Life doesn't stop because you're orthodox.

Only connect, said someone bent
on probing creativity's mystery.

I'm only reading casually so—
No excuses, please—a voice bullies me
to order: you're a poet, aren't you?
Try connecting.

And so I do. Try, that is,
twitching the mind's slack elbow.

The pie's distracting, succulent
rich and brown, so unabashed.
It's what it is.

I tell myself no faculty
was ever sharpened on a pie,
no complacency ever flattened either.

Leave it there.
Let the connections connect without you.
I say this to the one who's eating.

The pie is a synthetic whole,
ripe sonata of crust and meat and crust
baked to rule.

No mice.
No rubber bands.
It's 1989.
Three neat movements, there it stands.
Don't think.
Keep eating.

I pour red sauce to break the synthesis,
tomato scherzo.
Joy to balance melancholy.
The season needs a lift.
Four movements now.

Ordinary experience outwits
your analogues with other arts.

Imagine looking at a painting:
a pie is on a table, nothing more.
Acrylic on canvas, neat as pie,
Hockney maybe.

He'd call it *Pie on a Table*.
If he painted himself eating it
he'd call it *Man Eating a Pie*.

He wouldn't call it *Self-Portrait, Nurture* or
The Last Supper which might smack of
egotistical sublimity, claim spiritual
aspiration or a literary humour.
These do not exist.
And if they do, they're only a
projection of our needs.

Needs are for children.
This is adult viewing.

If Andy Warhol took it on
there would be fifty in rows of ten.
50 Meat Pies he'd call it.
Titles aren't the artist's bag.
Still Death would do as well
but never mind—the pudding's
proof enough ...

It fastens bluntly on your retina,
leaves your spiritual well-being high
and dry, our gold-brown flaky
high-rise pie humped with flocklets
of tomato sauce.
That's art enough.

It's not:

Little Jack Horner's individualistic self-
congratulatory pie,

or the king's hierarchic banquet, beaky
with blackbirds,

or the tragic moussaka of Thyestes
brimming with his children's gristle.

It is:

an Australian pie
legitimate ingredients
approved by Public Health,
no fancy foreign stuff—
we're Fury-friendly here.

Connections are taking care of themselves.
Our juices flow. Steam rises,
ribboning wisps in air.

In music, it wouldn't match
the *Grosse Fuge*, great C sharp,
nor the *Quartet in F* he polished off
at Gneixendorf: 'the name sounds like
the breaking of an axletree,' he muttered,
inner ear reverberant with connections.

'Muss es sein?
Es muss sein!'
Simple as pie, we say.

What is it then that *is*?
The pie steams open from its crusted skirts,
red gobbets sink below the rim.

If I were marrying music to this pie
I'd tie it to a wheezing barrel organ
from some innocent old carousel.

A crowd is gathering, nodding to
'The Road to Gundagai' and 'Come Back to Sorrento'.
Round and round the horses roll
their diamond eyes, stiffening
in full stride, biting the air
with wooden teeth,
letting it go at that.

For A.D. Hope

On the occasion of his 80th birthday

Past the open window
a sparrow flies, dips,

shuts its wings, drops
a little, spreads again

to lift   lift
catch itself rising.

Once, nervous, practically
invisible, I dipped into

your sight, pardoned
for whatever it was I wasn't.

Your dreaming head, freckled
delicate as a sparrow's egg,

charted the contours of
a shaky flight.

The lines seemed clear enough,
the hunters far away.

Kindness steadied the uncertain air.

I wrote a poem about you.
An anthologist thought it was about God.
A critical sleuth hinted at an absent father.

Forgiven still, the mind, listening,
catches a feathered rush of memory—

a little air
a clear pane
and a small bird
falling

Growing Up

When I grow up (I'm only fifty-five)
I want to be as mountainous and wise
as Marguerite Yourcenar.
A big stone sphinx
silent as a shadow.
The perfect balance between
grace and power.

I want to be strong enough to live
on an island off the coast of Maine,
let my beautiful garden run to seed,
receive an interviewer from some
prestigious TV arts programme
once every twenty years, descend
to read aloud with detached hauteur
prophetic passages from past work,
refuse the academy's accolades.

I will not miss my native land.
I'll know who I am.
My voice will be low, steady,
unemphatic, purged of need.
I will not mind being big-boned,
heavy. I will not notice
that my hair is thin,
that my eyes have come to a standstill,
that earnest questions stay unanswered.
The loss of lovers, children's defections
will leave me cold.

I will become the absolute
it's taken me a lifetime to annihilate.

Reading a Letter in Amsterdam

Under chestnut clusters looped in light,
a firm clean-painted bench.
I'm remembering you as you were before
we met, before I sat here with your letter,
waiting, watching children, joggers, lovers
pass, a blurred and broken line.

You've been away a long time
through all our pointless winters.
I've found you now in tenderness
like something lost in childhood,
remembering you as you were before
we met again, before I sat here waiting
on a bench in Amsterdam.

Like distant ghosts, older men and women
slowly pass the bench in silence. I watch unseeing
what's closer to me now than you,
remembering you as you were before,
as you might be now,
before your bright green spring
cut short our winter,
swam us into flower.

Your voice, a longing subterranean stream
has shaped our story, and your words,
those *words*, shake out like rain
in my cupped hands.

You are not with me.
I've come a long way to tell you
this reminds me of some other time,
some other place, but not the same
as what was lost in childhood.

Your letter's shaking in my green-veined hand.
I open it. Not open—
tear is closer to the truth, my hand
still trembling on a firm clean-painted bench
in sun-struck Amsterdam.

The Ballad of the Pretty Young Wife

for Helen Adam

Here is a tale of sorrow and woe
That happened in time so long ago.
An old man nearing the end of his life
Took to his heart a pretty young wife.

A wife to look after his house by the sea
His house forsaken and solitary
By waters dark, perturbed and cold,
The lair of creatures cruel and bold.

Through murky waves the sharks cut light
She heard their path in the dead of night.
She heard them gather, though far away,
And her will moved with them in search of prey.

'Be still, my dear, be still and sleep
Though the waters are dark and the waves run deep.
My little bride, there's no need to dread
The path of the shark in our sheltered bed.'

They hunger when only the easterly howls
Those starving sharks with their harrowing jowls
But when old age sags in a sleep profound
The cleaving fins make the only sound.

She dreamt that she swam in the rising wave
Naked and proud and young and brave,
She feared no sound, she scorned the dark,
Pursuing with joy the song of the shark.

Her fettered soul to its own kind sped
As she cleaved the waters dark and dread.
She breasted the waters so cruel and proud
At one with the sharks she sang aloud:

'I'm free at last to seek my good
I lust for my kind and for human food
And I hate the old man near the end of his life
Who welcomed me in as his pretty young wife.'

She dreamt next night of a knife-like fin
And the world opened up and took her in,
And she sliced through its waves like her kin, the shark,
And she lashed her tail when the moon turned dark.

'Show me the path on my quest for food.
Show me the source of life-giving blood.'
The moon came out from behind a cloud
And shone with force on the old man bowed

In the bed where he treasured the pretty young wife
The source of his joy, the jewel of his life.
She cries to the moon by the waters cold
As she turns in its light from the husband old:

'How can I yield to a husband's will
When the blood runs free and the sharks smell kill?'
But the moon turns dark and the clouds rush past
And the lives of the two are ebbing fast.

The very next night she climbs to bed.
The moon has vanished. She lifts her head.
'Are you coming, my wife, are you coming to sleep?'
'Yes, I'm coming. The stairs are so dark and so steep.'

He turns to his wife lying still in the dark
From her blazing blue eye flashes out a hot spark
Like a streak of hell's flame. He lies still as death
As she tosses and turns with her ravenous breath.

She pitches him down as his cries float to sea
'Alas for the monster my bed has set free!'
Tonight she is dreamless. Forever is he,
No longer she'll hunt with the packs of the sea.

For the pretty young wife has discovered her prey
In the arms of an old man who hastened the day
Of his sorrow and woe and the end of his life
When he took in his folly a pretty young wife.

Jacques Tati at the Darwin Hotel

Bonjour, words! Tell me where I am—
A thousand miles from everywhere,
they say.

Palm-fringed patio
a buzz of mauve, cerise,
pink and gold and green,
cascades of luminous bougainvillea,
frangipani fretworking
a weightless turquoise sky.

Mangoes drop their headlong smoothness
down the ropy vines, arched mangrove roots,
tangibles unlimited.

'Minimum dress for this area will be
SHIRTS, SHORTS, SHOES, LONG SOCKS'

The trustful waitress leaves me juggling
tiny plastic rectangles of butter,
marmalade, honey. I ferret clumsily
around the toast.

And there's the coast!

Improbable tall palms
a still metallic sea
and miles of sky.

People going out and coming in.
A boy is sweeping slowly up the path.

Here's a man with sideburns
short and chunky in his long white socks.
Determined.

He's carrying two large cases out.
The path is long, the greenery too frivolous.

And there's his wife. Her back is young and white
but she's not young. She limps to take a frontal shot.
They have to leave.

Her husband makes his second savage trip,
puts down the bags to help her with the light.
The boy is sweeping slowly.

It's hard so far away and she's unsure just where
the metre is. He shows her.
She snaps and snaps again. She's sorry
there's a satyr in the shrubbery
eating toast.

It won't be like the travel posters say.
But after all, a holiday's
a holiday.

Marius in Hobart, 1989

for Rosemary Dobson

Last night I saw an old French film.
A story told in black and white
about a woman's sacrifice for love.

Fanny, the little winkle girl
with shingled hair, gave up her
hope of cosy domesticity,
releasing Marius to his
South Sea island dreams.

It seemed both right and proper
back in Melbourne's old Savoy in the early 50s
before the soul's innocence was ironed out
that men fulfil their dreams
that women wait without hope
that magic sailing ships should come
and go.

Around the gentle pair clucked
hummed and growled a clutch of comic citizens
whose operatic gestures, male worldliness
about premarital sex we used to label
'French'.
Always shaping up and backing off.
No broken jaws, smashed skulls
or knives in backs. Only playing at it.
That was our world.

Rejected suitors took it in their stride,
never reached for guns,
got shrunk on couches.

Absurdly waddling Panisse,
a defrocked Alf Garnett with pointed shoes,
enormous bum, retreated graciously,
saw through his folly, growing
out of it, a momentary hero.
We breathed again for Fanny.

The men were fat and comfortable
in cummerbunds and aprons.
Enormous-bosomed women in respectable
black satin, no taint of sin upon its sheen.
All wore funny hats, drank wine at midday,
talking, joking on the generous pavements,
light airs teasing the loosened sails
in a peaceful harbour.

A rakish boater for young Marius,
abortive high-crowned Panama for the provincial
Lyonnais whose weedy moustache, fastidious lips
and twitching nose set him up for ragging.
Presiding over all, benign, absurdly tolerant,
sad-faced Raimu played Césare,
the widowed father.

We all wanted such a parent.
We thought they existed in France.
We believed in the forgiveness of sins.
There seemed to be plenty around.

But Melbourne wasn't Marseille
Sinister cranes
crouched over iron-grey warehouse walls.
The streets were empty.
The Savoy wasn't France either.
Other South Sea island tests
have taken place and a ship exploded
somewhere in a peaceful harbour.
Somebody else's.

So when I saw this old French film last night
I couldn't look.
The iron gates have shut.
It's too late to say you want to go back,
too late to say you've forgotten something.
You know you'd be lying.

New Age

There's a man on the radio.
He's being interviewed by a woman
with a thin holy voice.
Her name is Caroline. She's impressed.
The programme's called
'The Search for Meaning'.
He's impressed himself.
Between the slabs of self-
improvement vibrate slow harp
pluckings, 30s jazz.
He weaves a hairball round TECHNOLOGY.
She feels improved. Music helps
the ball go down.
'What was it like in gaol?' she breathes.
'Wonderful! It brought the holy monk
out in me!' He's ecstatic.
He tells her (twice) he grew
a beard. Goes on to say the beard
upset the governor of the gaol.
'No man in my gaol has a beard!' he roars
theatrically mimicking the governor's rage.
He has observed himself growing a beard
and found it good.
The interviewer ends her business
with a 'Peace Be With You'.
You can have him for $12 on cassette
at home.

You never know who's waiting for a spot,
dying to keep you quiet.

Miss Short Instructs Her Latin Class on the Fountains of Nepenthe, 1912

… Sparrowhawk
Steiner
Terribile
Titmus and, oh dear,
St Quintin, all here
and unperplexed.

Yes, the guide has just eaten
a raw crab *tremolo agitato*
but never mind; *la volonta di Dio*
and all that. We'll have a drink
soon and yes, Steiner, the rock
is indeed volcanic but the
mount quiescent.

Twelve fountains once,
according to Perelli—
some up high from
inhospitable rocky lips,
others jetting out from
vineyards, orchards
in the middle distance.
The rest near sea and shore.

Ancient healers praised them—
yes, in Latin, Titmus. Maybe
not like science as some
know it but empirical
empirical …
Good enough for Galen and
please, Terribile, put away
that frog. Providence supplies
no useless gifts, I know, but
we are not at home, however

evil-smelling. Restrain yourselves.
I know Greece was home to moderation
but is it too much to ask, Sparrowhawk,
that folly not be added to irreverence?

Faced by phenomena that seem
to mock the rational
be humble, Titmus. Yes, it *is*
the Mediterranean. The guide
is quite all right ...

Saint Calogero's fountain's what
he said and good for gout,
child-bearing, leprosy and,
if you don't eat lentils,
flatulence. Only sunburn,
Steiner. Your mother ought to
know that leprosy's extinct.
Varicose veins aren't your problem
yet, but ancients had them too.
Scorpion stings and other venomous
beasts—do watch your feet,
Terribile. The snakes are harmless.
I promised that I'd bring
you home alive ...

The Paradise fountain is
nitrous, Titmus. For distemper.
Farmers fattened up their pigs
and kept them glossy. No,
Sparrowhawk, the Odyssey
took place in Greece. This
happens to be Italy.

Hercules's Fountain proved to
be a laxative, tartaric and
could fix a harelip
vertigo and chilblains,

also a relief from piles the
universally misspelt
haemorrhoids—I see no
contradiction, Titmus.
No, *please*, Titmus, not
just now. I'm sure a little patience ...

This fountain known as
la Salina, mostly used
by women for unspecified
complaints. I said
unspecified and meant
it. Recommended also as
a sheep-dip. Let me finish,
Sparrowhawk. The Fountain
of the Virgin—what's so
funny now, St Quintin?

Purgative and blastopeptic,
gave relief from herpes
elephantiasis and
everything of atrabilious
lunatic disposition ...

Another which we won't pursue
today relieved the Babylonian
itch and other crudities,
fantastic visions, colic,
and affections of the heart
with which some of
you may later be
afflicted. I strongly doubt
that procrastinating
cataplasia was a raging
plague but you may
have something, Steiner.

The guide has told me
of another which, by
virtue of its smell alone
raised from the dead a
certain Anna Pasta lying
in her coffin. It wouldn't
even wake you up,
St Quintin, but try
to look intelligent ...

The Fountain of Saint Elias
soothes all who suffer
lechery and ingrown
toenails and no, Terribile,
please keep your
shoes on. It was never
dedicated to Priapic rites
no matter what you may
have thought you read.
The text was probably
corrupt ...

Grazie, the boat *per amore
di Dio*. Why should not a
fountain, Titmus, dry up
if it pleases?

III

Hospice Training

To get there, first you have to pass
the barriers of speech, unlearn
your hard-won plainness.

Is it worth it?

Pass a fence of iron spikes
raised to tear and gut what's crouched behind,
what's dying to get out.

Will it funk the course?
Will it survive?
Will it be free?

Open your eyes.
Try to look as if you're listening.
They're big on empathy here,
dull with concern for the terminally-ill.

I'm feeling murderous,
listening to the air explode
before their words put out the light.

I'm sorry but this is how it is.

When Lucia, Joyce's agonised daughter
heard about her father's death, she said:
'What is he doing under the ground, that idiot?
When will he decide to come out?
He's watching us all the time.'

That doesn't sound insane to me.
If you were ever a writer's child
you'd know the terror of a word
from the mouth of a primary carer.

They put her in,
these masters of language,
breakers of the whys and hows of a tale,
deciders of your fitness for the road,
who tell you how to mourn
and how to die.

But concentrate.
Try and forget the words.

Something delicate's alive behind the spikes.
Fix your eye low on that shuddering wing.

It has to be worth it.

Breathing Exercises

Have you ever tried to give your mother breath?

You stand, back to the wall,
a prisoner awaiting execution.

A bad start in life, you might say.
But whose?
We're not talking childbirth.

Desolation keeps you both in check,
as formal as white airless brides.

Her hands undo you, moving in
a slow blind caress,
arching over the clinical sheet
scrunched high in pain.

All you want to do is breathe
the panting mouth alive.
All you want to say, your chances
of being heard saying it,
left the airless room years ago.

Embarrassing scenes in enclosed spaces
were never permitted.

Gagged, you can't move.
Sentence has been passed
without words.

There are no bonds for good behaviour.

Afloat

I knew a father once
who when I said 'I want to fly a kite'
became for me a child again,
pretending not to know.

His fingers fumbled with the string
so mine should move more freely,
and everything was airy
blue and light.

In just such ways he taught my arm
a gentle arc in water, laughed me
into dead man's float
and porpoise flip.

Each day I waited for the toy-box
called an Austin
to rumble down the street
between the elms towards a
grey-green Melbourne sea,
jumping the running board
to ride that little strip of freedom
called 'our drive' before our mother
collared us to silence:
'Be quiet. Don't disturb your father.'

Would it disturb you now
to know I know what duty let you in for?
Or to tell you how, each day,
I wait that day's-end glimpse
of the whispering sea?

Call It Love

They met as prickly children do,
hiding nameless fears.

Their sad ironic faces
promised what they couldn't see.

When he died, she lay awake
an old photo in her head of a boy,
profiled against an apple tree in flower
staring out across the Zürichsee,
infinitely alone.

Curved solid with loss,
his young back shook tears out of her.

All their faltering life she'd hoped
to be a flowering tree for him.

You could call it love.

Reading

NO ALCOHOL: red ink across the page.
Why not, I wonder, hearing again
the social worker's words,
'They've come to die with dignity
so give them what they want.'

He's Kavanagh, James Brendan,
steady eyes, fifty-one years old,
a miner from the North, and Irish.
Dependents none.

It's in his lungs.
He sits up straight, alert and shy
his voice smoky as an old song.
'I haven't seen you here before.
You new?'

I've taken Edna's nip next door in 17,
faced Mavis, neck turned tight against the dusk,
who last week chucked her brandy over me
and cried. Both women with no visitors,
children somewhere …

'I'm new and so are you.
Your dinner's on the way.'
Eve might have greeted Adam so
in God's fine garden, not too bright
as usual, safe on lower ground.

His sheet reads, Cheerful, independent,
likes to talk.
                    The room is bare and clean,
no telly and no flowers,
a monkish radio, a phone.
No books.

'D'you read at all?' I ask who never did much else.
'I've never read a book, but I was fit.'
'I'll bet you were,' I say, thinking of
pitiless Dampier sand and sun that saps
the blood from a green country man,
loading his breath with dust.

His feet are swollen, stretched translucent,
the white V of his thongs still visible
between the sunburnt toes. I touch them gently,
wandering in the blossoming voice of this
mild solitary man. 'D'they hurt?'
'No,' he says, 'just the condition. Nothing.'

He knows his shape and substance without dread,
one who came and will go quietly
from this cruel country. My reading falls away.

'But let me tell you about yesterday,' he says.
I'm listening, Kavanagh, James, no alcohol.

'They took us to a play, just two of us.
I'd never seen one in my life before,
real people just like you and me!
We heard their squeaking shoes,
the floorboards creak. Word-perfect too,
remembered every line. How do they do it?'

O you, who never read a book
or hatched a child or left a wife,
your mother maybe half a world away,
why ask me that, absurd in Eden?

Unfit, I bend to touch his feet.
My hand shakes and he smiles:
'It's nothing. Really nothing.
Just part of the condition.'

Home Care

A rented one-room unit
right above the freeway.
Can you spare four hours tomorrow?
Just the usual—drinks, the toilet, company.
Her husband has to get away
to do some business. There's no one else.
They sold their house in Mandurah
to come to Perth. She's having chemo.
Seventy-five, mastectomy and secondaries.
Doing well, considering. One of our nurses
calls at ten. Her name?
How could I have forgotten—
Constance Bryant.

I've never done a home relief care stint before.
The coordinator's tone is flattering.
I'm scared, but I say yes, slow
to knock back chances these days
to apprehend an ancestor.
Anybody's.
Guilt, I think. I let mine slip away
when I was young and deaf
and indestructible.

Bert her husband's an ex-panel beater,
boyish in his seventies, trying
to keep things tidy. His meek front
speaks of order, devotion and
never a harsh word.
What I imagine might have been
had we been different.

He shows me tea bags, crackers,
half a chicken in the fridge.
Her tin of lemonade.

'Maybe she'll eat a bit of nectarine.'
'I won't.' Her voice comes strong.
'He's only happy when I eat,' she says.

Bert's stooped, pink, hesitant,
a mottled moon-faced innocent,
steel-rimmed specs, a checkered shirt.
I'm softening yet again to fall
for the heroic myth, the Happy Family.

Any children? Two.
A son in the army far away,
a daughter on a farm.
They can't get in.
Dad's looking after Mum.

The freeway hums below the balcony.
I'm watching tiny cars slide by in lines
like metal beetles.
Each one has a driver
going somewhere.

'I've brought a rose for you.
The only one alive from last night's easterly.'
Bert takes it gingerly, slowly finds a glass.
There's only one to spare.
'Thanks,' she says without her teeth.
Air whistles through the inverted U
of a pugnacious mouth, eyes flickering
back and forth.

He finds it hard to leave
worrying his bulk towards the bed
and back towards the door.

She's propped up looking hard at me.
She misses nothing, taking me back
to when my grandmother lived
and died with us, unschooled.
But sharp.
You couldn't fool her with a rose.

A hard life shaped that jaw
jutting above the sheet, a pale
blue nightie with its girlish trim
against the wasted flesh.
'Just show her where things are
and off you go. Give's a kiss.'
He does it all, awkward and slow,
finding the going hard.

'I expect he'll go to the dogs
when I'm gone.' She suddenly sits up
after the door clicks shut.
Her eyes have sparkled into witchery.
She laughs, grows larger in the bed.
'You see this table?'
Close beside the bed a little wooden stool
stands painted white.
She strokes the surface lightly.

'My son Gary made it for me.
Just a nipper in the primary he was.
We sold up everything. I kept this.
It's mine. Nobody gets it till I go.
I've left it to my daughter. Would you believe
that when I told *him* that
he suddenly got interested. Never was before.
They'll have to fight it out between them.'

Then she laughs again.
'I always wanted something of my own.
I grew up in an orphanage. He made it
just for me. My son did that.'

I sit beside the bed
but not too close, slipping
in and out of her mind.
I'm wondering how it feels to lie
inside an empty rented box
touching wood, how it feels
to know you're leaving
what might have been, what may be
or what never was.

She tells me that she's getting by.
'Time for a nap,' she says.

A mild wind stirs the curtain.

While she sleeps I'll read the weather
forecast, watch the bushfire's pall
above the freeway.
From that smile about her lips I'd say
she's off and dreaming.
About a homecoming maybe,
or just a small surprise for Agamemnon.

Soup and Jelly

'Feed Fred and sit with him
and mind he doesn't walk about.
He falls. Tell him his ute is safe
back home. Thinks someone's pinched it,
peers around the carpark all the time.
His family brought him in it and
he thinks it's gone.
He was a farmer once ...'

I take the tray. The ice-cream's almost
melted round the crumbled orange jelly
and the soup's too hot. I know
I'll have to blow on it.

Hunched, trapped behind a tray,
he glances sideways, face as brown
and caverned as the land itself,
long thin lips droop ironic
at the corners, gaunt nose.
The blue and white pyjamas cage
the restless rangy legs.
In and out they go, the feet
in cotton socks feeling for the ground.

'Are you a foreigner?'
'Not exactly. Just a little sunburnt,'
and I put the jelly down. I mustn't feel
a thing: my smile has come unstuck.
I place a paper napkin on his lap. He winces.
'You're a foreigner all right,' he says.
'OK,' I say. What's one displacement more or less,
wishing I were a hearty flat-faced Fenian
with a perm and nothing doing in the belfry.
Someone like his mother. Or a wife who
spared him the sorrow of himself.

Now he grabs the spoon. 'I'll do it.'
'Right,' I say, 'You go ahead. Just ask me
if you want some help.' The tone's not right.
I watch the trembling progress of the spoon
for what seems years, paralysed with pity
for his pride.

How does a dark-faced woman give a man called Fred
who cropped a farm and drove a battered ute
a meal of soup and jelly?

Outside the window, clouds are swelling
into growing darkness and there's a man
hard on his knees planting something in the rain.

In Memory, Vincent Buckley

1925–1988

> *Only the dead can be forgiven;*
> *But when I think of that my tongue's a stone.*
> W. B. Yeats, 'A Dialogue of Self and Soul'

Easy to say yes in winter
to a summer hope, the coming of a friend.

Another chance for two cold characters,
lately warmed, to take death's name in vain,
to laugh and maybe sing.
It seemed a simple thing.

Never exactly personal when young
we stood still, going places slow,
harnessed to whispering ancestors.
Catholic and Jew in a dumb and guileless country,
our heavens and hells were never shapeless.

Two solitudes with clever tongues
enough (we thought) to drown
the clamour of the coming night.
Short on small talk, stoned on
art's austere virginities, frozen in our
private dislocations (that's how you might have put it
once) stalking the metal-rimmed rhetoric
that once could turn a simple word like 'life'
to something as seditious as 'my body's occasions'.

We came to call it 'life', went on to live it
till our passing's halting breath became
too delicate to name.

You taught me Yeats's hardening into truth,
Joyce's defections. Their Dublin meeting flared
to life in class. Idealist and saboteur,
rootless high-class Protestant and petty bourgeois rebel
struck it rich for us.

Sometimes the body's occasions take on flesh.
Not rhetoric, but knives that slit the heart.
Nothing time's ironic surgery can't fix.

'I tune my muscles for the strait of death,' you said,
writing about the Persians in defeat, with maybe
Ireland's mayhem, murder in your mind.
'Life is a history of absences
And unprepared returns,' you said.

We don't know who we are when we are,
whisper the ancestors.
Before there's time to blink away your ignorance,
noble language springs the trap shut, earth tips,
and absence stares us back like dull grey stone.
And on that stone is written: there is no return.

We wouldn't dare to start a sentence now with
'Life is' anything
though gaudy Yevgenis of this world keep talking,
change their coats with every wind,
deform their tongues with dogma, answers for the
taking at their fingers' flick.

You said, 'Some poets are weathercocks, some
weather forecasters. For myself, I want only
to feel Jerusalem's weather.'
Surely a yearning mild enough for God
for all His clamour?

If mortality's a blessing, you are blessed,
leaving the song of yourself, the 'holy human'
to stretch us, tail you to the sacred city.

'Innocent, cocky, doomed,
Like a conman'—your words, old mate, loving
the ease, the frankness of American speech,
those blessed morsels of the ordinary,
rarer than ornaments of beaten gold and twice as rare
to those intransigent for truth amid imposture.

Occasions of sin
Occasions of virtue
spin into ribbons of air.

We go. All stays the same.

The timid seed pod of the heart
ripens to bursting in creation's fires.
Nothing time's ironic surgery can't fix.
Except a poem.

The past becomes an island of the dead.
Unready, nearly invisible, I swim around
in shrinking circles.

Like birds of benediction taking flight,
your words describe my path,
wedged in the buoyant wind:

'I walk beside these fires because I must,
In pain and trembling, sometimes thanking God
For what they give me, the few poems
That are the holy spaces of my life.'

For Jim

1947–1986

I

The minnow class swims in,
plaids and checks of older, innocent America.
Clear-eyed high jinks simmer to a stop.

These are the eighties. Jim is gone
who once sat sassy-tongued in class
learning the meaning of poems.

I'm in his home, alive.
He's dead in mine.
What's a poem now?
Nobody has a dime left to cry.

There he stood in plaid shirt and Afro,
lanky 26-year-old fresh from Ohio State in Western
Australia.
Hello, heart-string!

Have you practised so long to learn to read?
Have you felt so proud to get at the meaning?
What was all thaddabout? he asked, dying.

Shade stunts a crop, squinches a singer's voice.
I want to jump at the sun, he said.
I want to stretch my lip.
I want to be black, he said.
I'm here.

This was the morning of the day of the beginning.

Heading round the bend in the world,
returning to the loved and limber land he left,

I'm in America.
The minnows in my class today are black and white.

Is it because we love that we leave?
Or travel dust around the doorsteps we were born on?

Remember, he said, remember.

Fear not, be candid, said old Walt.
Dwell a while and pass on.
Be copious, temperate, chaste, magnetic.
But pass.

Jim dwelt a while, passed on, branded by unfamiliar light.
Home lacked the bold sunlight he craved.
Home lacked the bold energy he loved.
What is home? Where is love?

Remember with every leaf his coming.

II

After San Francisco, the pilot crackles out the States:
unfurling Nevada, Utah, Colorado, Oklahoma, passionate
peaks and sierras of the west passing,
passing Little Rock, Memphis, Chattanooga, and Atlanta,
passing over endless grasses, shrouded fields
snapped shut in snow
telling the copious tale of love in magic syllables, natural
as breathing: Okonee, Monongahela, Natchez,
Chattahoochee, Oronoco, Homosassa,
Seminole, Osceola, Econlockhatchee, Tuscawilla,
Moccasin Wallow, Slippery Rock, Apopka,
dropping in night down Florida's wrinkled nose
snorting the Gulf stream, the land charged, infused with
magic names, love's litany.

Did Yirrkala, Djankawu, Ngambek,
Mandogalup, Nyuninga, Kondinin
and Wallumburrawang seed Jim's enchantment too?
Sacred morsels of mystery, crumbs of divinity,
red men and black men stirring in their secret places,
dreaming in our yards.

Copious I break sprigs from the tree of death,
copious the yellow-speared grain rising,
copious the question: why?

God talked to himself in the mountains,
stirred from his platform in his secret place:
Folks ain't ready for souls yet.
De clay ain't dry.

And he sang creation's birth,
how seeds of earth and air, water and fluent fire
fused in empty space,
how gases burned, condensed, the land turned hard,
the seas rushed into place, stones took men's shapes
and all the creatures wandered in the hills.

He sang and laughed.
Death took his first taste,
tender grass being sweetest at dewfall.

III

Jim died, casually brushing by an *Eclogue*
while the catheter burst and merciful
morphine swam his head into silence ...

> *Like this clay growing hard, this wax melting soft,*
> *In the same fire may Daphnis feel my love's fierce blaze.*

> *For Daphnis I burn.*
> *Let my spells bring him home.**

The minnow class swims in and out.
These are the eighties.
Our feet are set wandering in strange ways.

> *Got on de train didn't have no fare*
> *But I rode some*
> *Yes I rode some.*
> *Got on de train didn't have no fare*
> *Conductor ast me what I'm doing there*
> *But I rode some*
> *Yes, I rode some.*

From Grand Central through the long dark tunnels out
out into highrise sunlight,
out by zigzag fire-escapes spidering the charred and
blackened Bronx,
cratered bombsites, car-hulks black and twisted,
New York's terrible backyard passing,
passing the battered spires, the appalled sky,
passing along the frozen Hudson crossed with strutted steel.
I see two blacks and a dog on the bank.
They pick their way through withered winter grasses,
blackness, wreckage. They stand a moment looking.
Snow clings to rocks at Spuyten Duyvel, Dobbs Ferry,
Ossining, Croton Harmon, the frozen river leading,
leaden sky darkening in patches, in strange cuts and jags
the ice is breaking up, and clapboard houses sink
beside the riverbank, the ranging hills, shadows of hurrying
tides haunting the river's reaches.

The song is passing, covering the earth, your country.
I am in your homeland, you in mine.
We are no longer innocent.

* This is a rough translation of Virgil's *Eclogue VIII*.

Well, he grabbed me by de collar and he led me to the door
But I rode some.
Yes I rode some.
Well, he grabbed me by de collar and he led me to the door
He rapped me over de head with a forty-four
But I rode some
Yes I rode some ...

Staving off old death with song,
Twenty-six years old you came.
Forty thousand years old and more you went,
giving in to chance and change, black boy,
rocked to sleep and slumber,
made and unmade by love.

Who put out the lie, supposed to last forever?
Love is when it is.
No more here? Plenty more down the road.
Take you where I'm going?
Hell no! Let every town furnish its own.
Who cares about no train fare?
The railroad track is there, ain't it?
I can jump at the sun, can't I?
I can ride blind, can't I?
I'm black, ain't I?

Darkness.
The brief and infinitely graceful dance of body,
fluid arc of upraised arms,
the dance in air, in empty spaces,
the rush to bite down,
all, all in beauty.

Remember, he said. Remember.

Black child, I will.
I do.

THE GATEKEEPER'S WIFE

The Gatekeeper's Wife

1

When a man died
My ancestors lit a candle.
It guaranteed eternal memory.

Severed from my ancestors
I light a candle for you
Every night inside a clay house.
Memory is only half the story.

2

You're always in my mind
Coming and going,
When I plant seedlings,
Helping me turn the earth,
Not saying much but kind.
I'm obviously a stranger.

3

The women were too strong.
You went away with all
Those struggling men.

4

I learned a gesture
From you, a slight
Turning away, a retreat
So little you'd hardly
Believe I noticed.

But it grew in me
Turned strong.
I had a force
Unknown before,
Maybe for evil.

It worked so well
You'd hardly believe
The woman I grew to be
Watching you
Turning away.

5

To whom shall I show
These early fronds?
They were planted
In your memory.

6

We seemed most lighthearted
of companions.
I should have been
What we seemed.
Were you what I thought
We seemed?

7

How did you say you loved me
For my apple-face?
The apple's bloom is gone.

8

Sleepless but alive
I talk to you late at night,
In early morning.
Where are you, I say,
Where?

9

Feathering a white thread
Through phantasmal waters
Your boat leaves me small
In dawn's first light.

10

Your mother said
My eyes were kind.
You never saw eye
To eye with her.

11

Come back, I've said
Many times hearing music,
Planting vines, watching
The dying sun.

12

Like an old familiar tree
I'm still here, your branches
Tangled in mine.

13

I call to you awake,
Asleep, still waiting
For an answer.

14

The steps of these poems
Are very small, your footprints
In my mind.

15

Touched by firelight, stretched
Through your young eyes
I found the best of me
The worst.

16

You had no memory, longings, home
No greed, truculence or idleness.
Speechless you mastered language.
Bent to that mastery
Behind a walled world
I stake young plants
In silent furrows
Always listening.

17

Maimed by compassion I
Set myself to learn your script,
Its beauty's fine edge lost
Passing through my hand.

18

Emptied of pity,
Another homeless dream
Lets you off in the dark
Candid, inflexible as always.
Foolishly I ask again what it was
I thought you wanted.

19

Not a character
But a destiny
Without a character
To endure it.
You can't revise a book
Severed from the possible
the suitable
the imaginable.
Someone is missing.

20

The gateposts of the house
tremble, candle falters
a sigh passing
passing over

Orpheus

These poems
with no point of view
are keeping you here trying
to answer
what might have been asked
what never was asked.

Your questions or mine?

Keeping the pen on the move
keeps you somewhere near.
It writes against our oblivion.

So long as there is a you
there is a me.
I have it in writing.

Death will come when you ask
and I stop turning back
to see who is asking.

Losing Track

Jerusalem in January.
A winter morning and my first time round.
Pink air, dark pines, stone upon stone.

The silent driver smokes: I watch
the climbing spiral of his breath as the van
circles steeply curving bends, the pine-soft hills

rising into timeless lightness:
a cold clear wonder of a day in Zion.
Zion! The very sound sets up a tranquil distance

from the self, an empty rounded space.
The eye yearns outward into history,
light rising on apocalyptic valleys, domes,

aspiring blurry harmonies of old and new.
Too tired to think, I'm watching and forgetting,
wondering how long can human memory stand

an absence trapped in strange geography.
The longing to return the dead to life dies
down at night, surges in early morning.

I'm losing track of your face in sleep, don't
know where you are, can't stop the clamouring flood
of other dead from breaking through.

Last night's dream had me struggling at a truckies' diner
buying food for you in Amsterdam, I think. Total strangers
everywhere; the usual tongueless bind, not knowing

where to take it, where you were. Others pushed and
begged but I was firm. For him, I told them.
It's for him. He needs it most. *We need it more,*

they shouted, grinning lipless over starving sockets.
Somewhere out there is a land, forgotten, promised.
No, neither promised nor forgotten but hovering

like a half-remembered voice in eerie stillness
between dream and waking. This is the place, this
the breaking country, the shattered valleys of Zion,

the place it has to be, knowing all the while
it's not the place. My body doesn't know where
it now belongs, not knowing where you are.

My memories are refugees who've fled beloved homelands
past return, terms never finalized, revolvers belted
ready, watchful, imagining annihilation.

Let's call it yet another confrontation with the past
in different air—not sacred, not profane, but different.
You might say getting close to God without God.

Poems and Things

Yad Vashem, Jerusalem 1994

In the eleventh century
Wei T'ai has told us how
a poem concentrates upon the thing
the better to convey the feeling.

Be precise, said wise Wei T'ai,
about the thing
but reticent
about the feeling.

When the mind responds, connects
with thing, the feeling shows.
This, he says, is how a poem
deeply enters us.

If poet puts his feelings down
that overwhelm, keeps nothing back,
he stirs us superficially,
says Wei T'ai from

eleventh-century darkness.
The poet keeping nothing back
can't start the hands, the feet
involuntarily waving, involuntarily tapping,

can't strengthen morality,
refine culture, set heaven and earth
in motion, call up necessary
spirits of the dead.

These are a poet's attributes
according to the wise Wei T'ai
who speaks from out of
ancient darkness.

Today at Yad Vashem
I visited our twentieth-century
darkness and I ask Wei T'ai again
what is a poem, what a poet,

hands involuntarily stilled,
feet frozen, eyes appalled
before a heaven and earth
once set in fervid motion.

Campaign Instructions

It is war.
The poets are losing
the children are crying
the mothers are leaving.

Upstairs a drum base is throttling
each poem's pulse.
Guitars impale us like bayonets.
Give us what cuts, burns, fouls,
every black thrust exact.

Out in the street a jackhammer
smashes the asphalt, deserts invade
the Amazon forests, images
stutter and fail.

Give us clubs and syringes
let light be thunderstruck
pity us.

Coronaries arson and sirens
vandals bruisers and bashers
arteries jetting from man-holes
jugulars gaping

the underworld's rumbling upward
the river soars red.
The poets go on seriously reading sestinas.
They are losing.

An old woman waves her bag rustling
plastic marches up front shouting
'Poetry sucks' as the poets cringe
behind their villanelles.

Come into that silent corner
where shade is alive, where words
ride air like dust in a light shaft,
where poems spin and furl upward
advancing invisible armies.

Roll the stone to the door.

What Fills

for R.A.

Your fluid probing poems
feel around the mysteries of process,
take on its origins,

now in focus, now a blur,
just as remorseless children
size up their creators,

hit and miss the mark.
We, the passive catalysts,
shameless chameleons,

colour ourselves to match
whatever's hiding.
Our colour is grey.

Crystalline water moves us
into green, to blue.
We wash over sleek rocks

black as burnt reptiles,
our obstructors and liberators,
lulled and jarred to shapes

of pain and pleasure. We make
imagination's depthless spaces.
What fills to breaking is

a soundless tide, rising falling
silent. Words hunger for us,
cannot find us.

Call it poetry.
Others do.

Banksia blechifolia

I.M. Primo Levi

Colourless, odourless,
no use or beauty,
why would you look?

My roots gnaw concrete
strangle cement, my razored
serrations protect the raw nub,

mute hollow of my plant heart.
You can't fathom my ancient
plant tongue, man speaking

to men. Neither daffodil nor
delphinium, poets project
no soft transports from

my fire-forged speech.
Barely exotic since I'm born here,
bearer of crueller histories

than your burning fields recall.
Seeded by typhoons, I've waited
years to raise my barbed and desperate

flower, colourless, odourless
and armoured. But reaching
reaching always skyward. My way,

you might say, of letting you know
death's around and ready. Listen.
You'll catch his passing breath.

Triple Exposure & Epilogue

The Caller*

(Gerhard Marcks, c. 1920)

Bronze brother, wild face lifted skull-like
in a howl, gaunt elbows stretching taut
a monkish robe, hands cupping anguished cheek-bones,
wasted frame past prayer. *Ora pro me*

Your name forgotten on the sandstone wastes,
back turned to towers of chrome and glass
far from the lost homeland. Instruct me in
your wordless patience, stilled ferocity.

Your homeless stance prophetic yet your words
remain unspoken mouthing pain of a God unsighted
sightless in this land of garish failure;
where is childhood's strict and wrathful judge?

Brought up hard against a stony tribe, nothing
I'd been taught or told prepared my way among
these people, brother: their stunted lingo,
shit and blood, their hardness.

They make a go of it, some tough core keeps
them at it. Do you give in, conform, do things
their way? Or wait to let the music take its time
to surface howling, stifle in your throat?

* *Der Rufer*, bronze, by Gerhard Marcks (1889–1981), stands in the forecourt of the State Art Gallery of Western Australia. Marcks has been called the 'last of the original German expressionist sculptors'.

Prompt me, brother. What is required of me,
long failed, who once craved silence
stillness timelessness? Obedient and rebellious
to what end?

Facing fading light, as scared as any time-bound
creature of the coming dark, the whispering grasses
close to the river's source, the half-heard music
staved against the promise of love's burden.

Something has to die behind the eyes for music's
reclamation from the mutilated spirit, for poetry's
release from silent rock, from watchful sandstone,
crumbling air, wind's sweep over grass. It can't be
forced but, like the sparrow's fall, will come.

And you will stand against the night, stretched
above stone, sightless sockets staring at the void,
at Him the Absent, body clenched against His wind
still waiting for a sign from home,

the weary echo of your cry closing inward
like the hurtling desert boomerang that circles
ever circling in subtle silent rushes.
O hear O *Ora*

Bride Drinking from a Pool

(Arthur Boyd, 1960)

Who is she?
Dragonfly wraith,
white child tilted headlong
floating sus-
pended, blind pebble eyes
dive a dark hole.
Why are her overblown
wingsleeves splayed
groping miasma's rim? Why
such swollen spider spatulates
for a puppet-hold on nightmare?
Whose is this haunting?

Who's watching this
plummeting sleeper?
Trapped between sky and water,
you're spotted by a shady duo:
inky crow's swivelling topaz eye
pimps for his babydoll cockatoo,
scared as a soul adrift, parrots
your bridal plunge down to the
reptile kingdom secret with
savage totems. The spectral hooks of
burned trunks grimace like sickles.

Bride,
        where is your epithalamium?
Your dove-mother mourns, falling and
fumbling, a barren tree stunned
into silence.
Why has the groom forsaken his dark one?
Why banished his flying fool?
Were you unclean?
Do you lie unreachable, fail to plant

joy in his bed?
Did your creeks and gullies dry
at his touch?
Did your spider clasp terrify?

Pitched from the cradle,
rocked with the motion of mourning,
the veiled pupa hovers inches above
her dark mirror, eyed by insouciant crow
flashing his cool, cocky drag-queen
in tow, fellow-travellers in flight.
Call it a bird's eye view, turfed out
to risky air to end hanging
headlong in a dead wood.

Bride-haunted,
your own face is thrown back
larval in the pool of exile. Without
hope of reward you reach down
to drink, trusting
to be fed.

Portrait

(Louis Kahan, 1992)

Though they lived for years in the same town,
they met later as strangers.
The poet asked if he would draw her in his 87th year
for her book jacket.
Businesslike he agreed.

And although he is older than she and famous,
they are both of the same archaeological stratum
marked Tough, crossers of many bridges in
countries marked Entrance or Exit.
Their pasts have intersected unknowing.

He once knew her late mother, a formidable judge
who went at things head-on, said he could
show them a thing or two about drawing and died
knowing what's what.

The daughter's different.
Not to understand's her goal, out of key
with the sublime. She knows a lively line
on sight, knows gorgeous language lies,
that the oppressor's tongue can lure, seduce,
that art is a compulsion to mastery.

Men watch women.
Women watch themselves being watched.

She has always been the watcher,
seen the scars, discolorations, damage, loss,
creeping arthritis, middle-class teeth scraped
twice a year. Paying attention
to lifelong facts her lot.

Despite the facts she doesn't know the score.
It seemed an easy thing to do, to sit
and let the master work his miracle,
humming away over the black pots and nibs,
the sunny room, the light, the harmless ease of it.

Not aiming to convince, she sits at his request
on a high stool, focuses on a metal figure in the window,
slips easily into silence crystallized
as still as Lot's wife.

He sits her high in semi-profile, assesses contours,
facial planes, the angle of the jaw, powerful surge of nose,
the peering eyes like some tranced visionary.

Why then now it is done does she feel floodlit,
targeted, consumed and wrung? Her feathers skewed
and draggled, heart a muffled drumbeat,
her own cortège.

That's wonderful, she says aghast.
Too much dying, too much growing up in that face
she thinks, that's my grandmother she says going on
to spot her father, mother, a couple of sisters
and an aunt. Where's she in all this family webbing?
'They see their ancestors before they see themselves,'
says Lily who has seen it all before.

The poet's not quite ready for that weighted face.
Is anyone ever ready for exactly who they are?

She's a strong woman, he says, adding a hint of bitterness
to the mouth. She's a good woman, he says, with kind intent.
Oh no I'm not, she thinks, I'm weak and cowardly.
Who is this stranger that will front her book,
trying to recall her younger self before
she was torn from sleep into this remote, severe
and sorrowful mourner and mother?

Cues from others' definitions:

Do I look old?
Very well, I'll be old.
Do I look wise?
I'm not, but for your sake—
Don't be fooled. I'm slow and stupid.
Or have you seen what's hidden all this time
and I'm the last to know?

The way we see ourselves,
the way we'd like to be can never fit
the artist's bill who forces you to flower
to fruit before you know what's what or
who is watcher, who is watched,
like God, beyond forgiveness.

Epilogue

Wiping the Canvas

As if we started like a gasp in the heart
of an unseen artist moving supple
between oil and pen.
No permission asked, none granted.
A stroke here, dash there, symptoms
surging into being; the long vague wash
of indeterminate blue, shouting blasts
of red and ochre.

Half asleep, we catch creation's rustle
hum and bang, afraid to answer
to our likeness. A daily fear,
mind and breath out of gear in buzzing air.
We gasp before the process of
our own creation.

Not allowed to peer too close,
some cheat, complain about the haze,
the blur, the thickness of the paint,
the lack of focus. A quick glance here,
a wink, no questions, please.
We're entertaining stillness.

Suddenly the canvas has been wiped,
the brush strokes stop and start again,
we think we've seen ourselves in innocence
absolved, obscure.

We try to bolster confirmation
from indifferent strollers, learn the
meaning of a work in progress from the hints:
a casual frivolous dig, the sympathetic twitch,
blurt of rage, censorious whine, indulgent
purr are all we have to give us definition.
How we rate, unseen, unlived, hang on such
flimsy stills.

Do, but also seem, say the sages.
What's invisible is useless.
Reason's demeaned that doesn't wear
a reasonable face. The image that you
think you are, the face that's happening
right here, stops short of what's projected
on that bare wall over and over
and over and over
                        and
                         O

Finding Focus

For Vivian Smith

Coeval in the indices, arriving safe
the year that Hitler came to stay,
our taking-off looked on a small
coherent world, a settled continent.

Taught silence when not saying yes
to what was asked of us,
what was allowed, death took only
oldish folk and people 'in the paper'.

Teachers, Argonauts both (I was Hesperides 29
in '44), I'm sure your poems made the
Dragon's teeth, the magic Fleece, always
well beyond my hazy grasp.

You found your focus early,
trusted your path in streets
ending magically in water.
'How some themes return,' you said,

Remembering the 'pathos of the past,
the human creature'. Growing up near water,
freedom's pledge, beckoning ships protected us.
I see their masts' geometry clear as yesterday,

sails lowered, waiting for the world's winds,
recall your quiet voice in poems scanning
clouds advancing, flickering light on water
reflecting back our patient generation.

Learning

What the teacher couldn't know
has taken half a life to learn,
classes of the troubled seventies
probed all her ignorance of life,
of poetry, wrenched aside her fiercely
focused paranoid love.

Recalling distant voices, learns that
yesterday possessed its sense and motion
like today. And all the other days
praised ruefully now more alive
than ever she expected. If someone came
to ask *how have you spent your life?*
she might let on where teaching took her,
what cross-fire illusion triggers,
what the rewards of ignorance.

That fair-haired boy so meek and mild
who seemed to grasp what Yeats intended,
repossessing silence with passionate intensity.
He turned a crooked alderman, ripped off the old,
condemned the young, made fancy speeches with
conviction, shot his wife and had a go at mum.
The dreamy chrysalids bore dragon-seed, and
yet again wrong-headed gleaner got it wrong.

Her brightest star, all nerves and brain,
soared on to Oxford, dazzled them on Woolf
to finish raging in a silent nunnery,
getting by with Jesus. Then cursed the teacher
for her life, rained tracts against carnality
upon that slumbering fuddled head believing,
severed, worlds were set alight by candid lyric
verse like Herbert's Love, bade welcome to
the unworthy soul only to reap a legacy
of dust and madness.

Another of her genius boys could never meet
a deadline, wrote on Wordsworth only, slowly
slowly one dead letter at a time, pressing
his anguished pen through paper till it bled,
ending somewhere in a Poona ashram shaved
and anorexic, preaching holiness to dogs,
the precipices in his head ringing through
darkness, teacher still half in love
with words that tinkled like iron.

But there were others. Each year some
new light broke in flashes of deliverance.
A brooding restless gypsy of a girl whose
dark resistant glance told teacher she was
anywhere but in a musty classroom picking
over poems. Unsure, impulsive, hinting
hidden grief, not all that keen to be too close
to Yeats. Maybe she knew the curse pinned
on his daughter wishing her plain.

Privileged by poetry, the teacher weathered cave
-ins, crises, serious doubt, walked through walls
the journey halfway over. *Purgatorio*'s similes
scooped her from the edge to calm. The emperor's
metronomic nightingale kept nightmare under
wraps. The boys and girls outflew her life
to sprout new sets of feathers. Had she wasted
their time? Her own time on the skids, steadied
for a lone spell in New York, waited among
random whispers of mortality.

Alive to all the chances of that ticking marvel
of a city, teacher warmed herself off the page.
Like a crazy parent cloaked by students'
exploits, took to fitful sidling squatters in
downtown tenements, hailing psychos mumbling

towards upper Westside rooming houses, Cuban
needlestickers, scavenging Salvadorean *anarchistas*,
high rolling ghetto-blasting blacks on legs
like stilts, rainbow flashers.

Sakura Chaya sushi, endless coffees, diner checkout
repartee, the Gothic plays of Christopher Street,
flick sessions screening Dylan's life and women,
past-midnite marathons in hooded fleapits, weaving
cross-campus 2 a.m. behind a pulsing blue buzz,
light from a little patrol van. The racing heart
came good under that high sky, between flaky canyons.
Coasting on bravado, teacher kept herself at arm's
length, stayed close to life to letting go
among lives as short and absolute as a heartbeat.

To live it up and frisk New York, what days!
Now former lives take over through all her
dwindling summers, catwalking in memory
the freshly fallen snow …
Light as a cat, today she prints a golden eye
on the good world quickening, children messing
in the earth's sweet mulch, alive to every knot
of time that once spelled happiness.

Without adjectives to reckon how
verbs to work out why
nouns to know what
learning the new heart's tenses,
surprise concordances, and how O
how not to fear the fatherless dark.

Café Sitters

never make decisions in their lives.
Take my hairy pal, Morton Figbloom,
glimpsed at distant tables waving
casually to past and sometimes
present friends. Hi, Morty! Eyes
shunt inwards, gives a languid nod.
Today he hardly knows me.

Standing long enough at crossroads
one path always proves impassable.
Always two women on the scene:
one knocks him back,
one kidnaps him, incendiary
with salvation.

Always two careers afoot:
one of them falls through
something happens somewhere else
someone from the old days makes a date
someone leaves a note
in an uncollected bottle—

Some hint at calculated ennui,
others heartbreak, loneliness.
Yes, Mort's a born café creature,
claustrophobic desultory prowler
going interestingly nowhere, confabulating
reworked novels, song or two, who to phone,
where to eat, what to do, when not
to do it, one hand on an imaginary gun.
You think you hardly know him? Today
he seems to have forgotten
that he thought he knew you.

Letter from Claudia in the Midi

I used to shoot in Kenya.
You'd never think I started life as Muriel,
forty head a day, a hundred cartridges:

zebra, wildebeest, marabou,
jackal, wild boar, leopard,
the largest birds alive.

I know you don't approve,
stuck in that boring place,
all that sand and miles of sky,

missing your indifferent kids.
Still writing poems are you,
way above my head?

You were a weirdo back in school,
your nose forever in a book. You tried
to ape my nerve but even when you jumped

the moving tram, fell off. You didn't
even wince at those trite Colombian candlesticks
I sent you when you married.

Or the witchy card, 'Congratulations!
It's a Baby!' on your first. We can't
all make the team.

The blackbird's song's seductive
and my voice has dropped an octave,
Gérard says, 'Tu deviens homme.

I'm off to Paris for a week.'
'Get lost!' I say. My handyman
takes pot-shots at the olive trees.

His sons are savages and want their lunch.
I scream abuse and burn their traps
laid near the kitchen tiles.

The cats are watching me. Gérard's
a swine. Mushrooms sprout around the oaks,
those little yellow flutes push up

the moist dark soil, pink hoods are rising
under the umbrella pines. There's singing
from the valley, the yearly fête, and

open trucks piled high with glistening grapes
are trundling past. The countryside is rank
with harvest's sweet sour smell.

I drive to Grimaud every day, car open
to the wind and pass Alain the handyman
rearing like Ben Hur behind his truck wheel.

'Ça va?' he shouts, 'Ça va?'
and I shout back, my deep cracked voice
vanishing in the wind.

Neither of us cares. Sometimes I drive
to Beauvallon, a sickle-shaped white beach,
cool off in water swept clean by the Mistral,

small yachts offshore, sails billowing
down in slats. I'm hardly visible these days
in 50's bathing gear. If some hulk's eyes

hover round my way, they settle on some
plumpish *poule* or anorexic pout left over
from the tourist season, topless on the sand.

Pig-tailed blond, piquant brunette,
not here to swim. The passing men will turn
and smile, even with wives in tow.

Midday, and they all clear off. What bliss
to be alone with all one's ugly thoughts:
how old and despicable one has become

compared with Françoise, Éliane, or Rosie
(Gérard's latest). Beach-bored I wander
barefoot to the car, relieved my hair has

bleached without peroxide even if the poor
old skin has lost its sheen, no longer golden,
with a pouch or two. But you're above

such things, writing your life away
under that clear blue sky. I like your letters
better than yourself. You say you welcome mine.

We both have tigers in the blood. I shoot
at mine and miss while you put yours to sleep.
Death's toughening, softening us for dust;

you shocked by me and I laid waste by you
is kid stuff to his watchfulness, the biggest
tiger of them all. Back home, the table's laid.

Pain de campagne, butter, great hunks of Gruyère,
tomatoes straight out of the garden. I'll start on
Château Neuf du Pape 1964, the year they tied my tubes.

How delicious it will taste when drunk alone.
Write soon. Can't promise to reply but then
I never could keep promises.

                Your ever-unreliable
                and charming friend

Claudia

On the Acquisition of Four Famous Chinese Novels for the Senior Library & Related Matters

How do you keep a young man
sitting in the spring?

Someone has heroically reviewed
a reading by a poet with a spiky name.
Her picture stares forbidding
into space, some mad old bat
who came one night and carried on.
What she knows wouldn't get you
far in economics.

A more seductive lady of the Qing
smiles slyly in the broadsheet margin,
eyebrows quizzical, her mouth a slivered moon,
her layered skirts a promise of decorum,
a grace undreamt in Queenslea Drive.
Her hands are raised and curved so gently.
Is she dancing or repulsing an advance
or something hidden from us in the tides
of history?
          When I say no I mean it
but I never shout.

No margin for that error in the Qing.
How do you keep a young man
sitting in the spring?

Is this what Kah Keong Yip and Khong-Shin Chia
both Year Eleven meant when recommending
'glimpses into Chinese culture'?
And what, I wonder, did Tom Flett really say?
I'll bet his heart said something other
than 'a good idea to broaden knowledge
of the student body.'

That's someone else's tongue, a Keating or
a Court, devisers of war strategies and tactics
so easily adapted to computer games,
computer minds.

I like to think the fearless funny Monkey*
gets top billing, refuses adaptation
to computer, shepherds on his lonely monk
through fen and forest armed with cunning
and the power to charm, disarm with human words
and finally turn in among the fallen leaves
of Queenslea Drive to welcoming friends.

There's more to culture than a useful acquisition
as any dancer in the margin tells you,
gentle hands mysteriously raised
against the tides of vanished dynasties,
no margin left for error.

---

* From the classic Ming Dynasty novel, *Journey to the West*, in which the Monkey hero whirls his staff and vanquishes demons ten times his size.

Shelley Plain

On the occasion of Shelley's two hundredth birthday, August 4, 1992

Of all that wayward lot, he's with us still.
His brother singers blissfully dissolved
In Lethe's stream, reneging on the thrill
Of protest, schisms of life and art resolved.

High voltage rock star, bongo-backed, offloading sparks
And ashes, chanting his 'Masque of Anarchy'
To the zonked. The press give him full marks
For political correctness; androgynous creativity

Boosts him high with feminists. Not strong
On history, they're unaware of Fanny,
Claire, or Harriet drowned, of Mary, long
On patience, short on sense, the many

Children (six or seven, half dead). Dons congregating
At Lerici, rear in panting jargon
Archetypes and cultural totems, propagating
Further pious cant. He's far gone

From all that crap, once sent down for pamphleteering.
His Oxford college held a ball in June
This year. Black tie affair, the ticket nearing
Eighty quid, dance bands, champagne, full moon.

For ten pounds couples posed for snaps before
His marble monument coiled with sea-nymphs weeping
By E. Onslow Ford. Outside the door
The unemployed, unruly vigil keeping,

Yelled and spat beside the Shelley-in-Italy pizza stall,
'He was an anarchist. These people kicked him out.'
The West wind gathering violence round the swirling hall
Foretells two hundred further years of drought.

Groundswell for Ginsberg

> *Always be ready to speak your mind,*
> *and a base man will avoid you.*
> William Blake, *Proverbs of Hell*

Nothing speaks louder than unwritten poems,
battening down silent grief our first suffering's source,
yearning branches poisoned at the root unleafing
leaf by flimsy leaf.

Built-up charges of th'unburdened heart still earn
acclaim: wise, funny, subversive, artful, cool.
You think so? Some price to pay for an approving blurb.

Well, not tonight artful, not tonight cool.
Absurd maybe. Rash, but not for some time cool,
dry-eyed suburban sibyl mad-mouthing groundswells.

Take Wordsworth's emotion recollected in tranquillity.
I'm feverish with what's not tranquil, what's been
settled for. What's a word's worth?

Pretending to be selfless mouthpiece, pottering
lake and fen unfurrowed, closed, serene, pitying
luckless leech gatherers, ditch dwellers,

mourning industrial mayhem unstoppable.
Man speaking to men meaning bush-whacker extraordinaire
meaning Himself—which men

had he in mind? Not Blake
or Ginsberg or me for sure.

We don't live in the Lake District
among rural men, rural come to think of it
women, or ballads with a tribal beat.

New York, London, not. Here's serious shortage
of tranquillity enough, a country with as many
souls as Wordsworth's England, 1801.

Better to be the perishable fly in this equation
to Wordsworth's slumbrous spider crouched
to stun emotion to tranquillity.

Were I only Allen Ginsberg sardonic with poise,
humour and humility of the 70-plus survivor
of 70's America today your ears would prickle.

I'd haul a wheezing squeeze-box on my lap,
chant hot poems of death straight off the slab,
cordon recollecting Willy right off the map.

Sing out supercilious William Buckley Junior
flashing ferrety fangs on his own telly spot,
priming his acolytes to mock the compelling voice,

deride with polite applause, uneasy titterings,
mad Orpheus hymning his dead, his wrecked
mescalin fired-up generation,

push back the tides of his passion
with mincing American teeth, the human face
a furnace sealed, the human heart its hungry gorge.

No point writing when the spirit doth not lead
said Ginsberg following his Blake, tenacious,
vulnerable, persisting vision straining heavy lenses

through fogs of unseeing 90's America where blight
still cuts the tender corn. Ginsberg's a professor
in a suit, once expelled from the academies for crazy,

happy-not yet-to be a corpse, Orlovsky, Kerouac, Cassady
dead, acclaimed as wise, funny, subversive, artful, cool.
Life's price paid for such a blurb no next-time round.

Remember 70's Ginsberg, old courage-teacher.
Remember his battered squeeze-box blowing out the bone song,
decades of getting ready for God.

Blake rages beckoning from the whitening furnace.
We face the night, half-mad with pity like our agitated
blasphemous mothers running to defend us hapless

with drawn swords, resented for what they were
ready to lose, for what they had already lost,
for what we in anger retrieve in their holy name.

> *The key is in the sunlight in the window*
> *the key is in the bars, in the sunlight*
> *in the window ...*

Remember through the bars John Pat speechless
in solitary sunlight, imagine the floating white
strips of sheeting, the innocent shoelaces.

Imagine our hopeless children shredded
by speeding metal, shorn field flowers
in the blighted corn, city of angels.

Listen last to barred black Angeleno Olin,
Larry, jailed for life for stealing—never speechless
in America—two pairs of trousers, forty dollars' worth—

Between the bars the sunlight in the window,
somewhere the key ...

> *Has the world gotten crazy or is it me?*
> *Am I so terrible at this thing called life*
> *that they decided to throw me out of the world?*

The real language of men. Cool.
Man speaking to men and maybe women in a
serious shortage of tranquillity.

Forget the tellers. Remember the tale
and the frail ghosts of our passing flowers.

Peminangan*

caught
on foot
through the window
of a car moving
slowly up Jalan Dago,
your head high
on a young neck.

caught
on a straight road
between a saunter
and a march,
the disciplined line
of your back
slanted towards hope.

you didn't see
a girl watching you go,
behind glass,
travelling slowly up Dago,
caught by a sudden shaft
of sunlight, bend
towards the pane

* *Peminangan* – 'courtship' in Indonesian.

Perdjodohan*

Set in your father's European suit
wide-lapelled and hairy blue
you seemed so delicate—
I loved you for the courage
in your bones.

I floated loose
in Mrs Pronk van Hoogeveen's
rumpled linen, several sizes past
my own, incongruously remembering
my father's lady on the side
and, casually, how Mrs Pronk looked
something like my mother.
But this was not the time or place
for others.

A trail of moon orchids dangled
down the water-cooler's fins;
my hand was trembling on the stem.
Hold on, you said. *We're off.*

I held you fast, the orchids flew
behind, a knot of scraggled *ayam*
leapt and scattered in our wake,
bombed-out feather dusters clucking
huffs of winded dignity.

I hugged you laughing,
relieved your profiled lip
had twitched into a porpoise curve.

---

* *Perdjodohan* – 'marriage' in Indonesian.

Newly married! Newly married!
sang the motor bike to dust
puffs rising from our dash.
We were, and how I wished to be.
Why then do I remember,
thirty five years on and stubbornly
alive, how in Djakarta once
I looked into a mirror,
tying back my hair deliberately
beautiful as any tireless mermaid.

White ribbon just in place when
Mr Pronk van Hoogeveen stepped close
to fasten in upon my eyes
glowing with possession:
You're going to ruin your life he said.
The jasmine-scented air closed in.

I tugged the ribbon tighter
tossing back the tumbling switch.
And leaning to the mirror laughed
like one possessed of something
not yet owned or named.

Kera Kera*

Climbing steep to Lembang on the bike
through dusk freed from day's dank heat,
the cool was sweet on our skin our eyes
and sweet the scented air reverberant
with frogs, gongs. I gave up words, let
go like flights of small dark birds to
match your moth-like silences, my Western
outlines blurring and dissolving,
your dreamer on the dickie seat.

Tea-pickers of Priangan gone,
gone the *kerbaus* shunted stumbling home,
gone the *tukang*'s bent-kneed glide,
the bobbing poles, the whacked tin
kettle, coconut shell and drum
dying down to soft night murmurs
laced with burning needlepoints,
the fireflies' swooping nets.

We sat in the teahouse garden
under a tea-rose bower to let
the lower world cool off. Far down the terraced scrawls
thin films of mist filtered the dying light
into blue-mauve evening. An old black gibbon
kept an eye on us, our *air djuruk* thick with sugar.
Loose in a jumping crouch, swinging skinny arms
he hung about for what a human means
by time's rewards.

---

* *Kera* – Indonesian for monkey; *kerbau* – bullock; *tukang* – peddler; *air djuruk* – orange juice.

It grew dark fast. Black clouds blossomed high
over the Prahu rimmed by sunset's sizzling
orange fuse. I saw those running bursts, can
see them now alive in no particular order
alive in no special way alive
remembering how you used to say
it was getting to be time
to drink up and come home.

Akibat*

I said I can't imagine life without you
as the coconut man passed our window
tapping his shell in the dust

      toc toc   toc toc

I said I'd stay with you forever
as we ate our first meal by the window
(tiny *ayam*, beans and carrots), sunlight pouring in
on the terrazzo floor. The air so still,
the babu's brown feet splayed soft beneath her sarong,
smiles enveloping our joy.

Njonja muda tuan muda, she would chuckle
young Mrs young Mr—how could she know
that we were only children?
At our age she'd given birth to eight.

At night we laughed and rolled on rice grains
pimpling the mattress. She wanted to make sure
we'd have a child, young njonja and young tuan.
Outside the window the kebong's twig broom
whispered over gravel like a blessing

      sh sh   sh sh

You told the story of your ruined childhood
as if it happened to a stranger. I was torn
with pity under the hammer blows.
Ashamed for outliving you, I can't forget,
a long way from that house, that window.

---

* Akibat – 'outcome' in Indonesian.

Conference Hi-Jinks

A Summation

(Religion & Literature Conference, 1996)

Capricious ageing writer, four days
dead at sea in a symposium,
tell us your beads.

Modestly the poet stirs: maybe
a line or two? tart and shortish, never fear.
Too hot for God or poetry here.

Nothing fancy neither prop to papmongers
propagandists, purgatory purveyors,
incapable of heaven, lockjawed
poets make quirky guests at gabfests.

Too prompt with sideline snort and
sniff, aghast at having to share a loo
with younger, firmer scholars who
know where it's at.

Poets turn up after the Keynote Speaker's
seared the rafters, grumbling about the
weather having lost a wallet on the bus,
missing the one undoubtedly serious person
everyone's raving about.

The one who dashes continent
to continent pronouncing ecumenically
to large and reverential hosts
proclaiming the demise of that which
nobody dares name because—well,

let us not forget in these
terrible times in which we are
obliged to live, the need
to be silent.

Or alternatively in these
terrible times in which we are
obliged to live, the need
to speak out.
Or …

Poets drop off during after-
dinner speeches by speakers
almost as learned as
they wish to seem.

Not before (craving a smoke)
they've spotted meaty metaphors
from Heaney, Dante, Mandelstam,
the tribe of sanctioned dissidents,
wincing under heavy-duty grids:
Platonic schema, tessera, kenosis.

Snarky poets take God's name in vain
but so have others in more secular sense.
Ora pro nobis if You can:
can't blame You giving up on man.
He's given up on You.

Only one Thou left in all the world
that clerics nickname You.
As well that God was never dubbed
or he'd be Les or Mike or Dave,

obliged to haggle with a world
some rare birds know it's proper to grow wise in
if only that so many dead still rise in,
or happier still, rest quiet in the grave.

American Safety Valve

(AAALS Conference, Humboldt State University, 1996)

America, you hand me poems on a plate.
Back in massage-therapy land, they crowd
Push, pluck, bend, swerve at the static
Summer self, knock, break and batter
Down the stiffened neck, the stoic muscle,
Crack the jointed brain, send in whatever's still
Alive and wham the lock gates open,
Free the attic-bound deluded pacifist
Fresh from hosing down the lawns
On her volcano somnolent in W.A.

Remembering the Mexican-plucked lettuces
In San Francisco, thousand island dressings
In a thousand variants, another shredded salad
Takes me back to wharfside San Francisco
Young together in the sixties, father, mother,
Eight-year old enchanted kid.
O memory! O America!

Inside, the rooms alive with heat,
Water tumblers clinking ice, the peeling
Hotel ice machines, no global warming in Arcata,
Global warnings somewhere else—
Not in America, not in Arcata.
Outside, the still clear night.
Patient stars tick over the Plaza,
McKinley broods while someone somewhere else
Is whistling past the cemetery in the dark,
Another night, another day, another shot.

Earth churns through its relentless cycles
Once called God.
Not in America the changeless,
Urgent namer, finder of facts

Dear land of most precise delineations
Of disaster, hierarchic as steam engines
Electric particles tuned to the max,
Another shredded salad swamped in Roquefort
Mini pizza next to midnight take me back.
Inside the room alive with heat I'm breathless
Breathless in Hotel Arcata with the claw-foot
Bathtub, head straight for an arcane
Convection heater pulsing its coils under
Closed windows, fiddle knobs,
Wrestle seized valves till Whammo!
See the writing on the wall:

Do not touch radiator or turn or adjust
any valve.
Radiators only operate fully open.
Heat is regulated by timer.
If room is too hot, please open window
Until heat cycle is completed.

(Omigod how will I know when heat cycle
is completed? Who regulates the time span?
Does he or she or they know what's a decent
shift for heating furnaces? Quis custodiet?
Who fiddles by burning Rome?
Who's that crying from the furnace?
Stop in god's name. But more's to come.
You children, hush your lip and listen):

Steam may make banging noises if
Pipes are cold. If valves are closed,
Steam valve may separate from radiator,
Causing steam to shoot out.

(*Shoot out*, nothing less. What drama
in the prose. Violators will be cited,
bicycles destroyed, indefinite particles
ad infinitum ...)

Tampering with this radiator
Could cause burns or steam burns.
Yes and more precise than anything else burns.
So touch nothing.
Take it from us, we've got you
On our minds, our hearts.
You matter.
We care.
You burn.
You sue.
We really care.

Leave it till tomorrow then
to nut out reasons for not caring
that they care,
for a chance to tamper
with a valve,
for a chance at the nameless
the possibly unnameable.
As the Tao tells us,
Can a man cling only to heaven,
Know nothing of earth?

A Laureate Comes to Lunch

(Poets' Lunch, Perth, W.A. circa 1983)

Well, said Crow, what's the booze?
A mediocre Riesling, I'm afraid, said God.
Crow laughed.
He bit the cork right off.

Speechless with qualified admiration
God passed another bottle.
Not every day the Word failed Him.
Crow's strong teeth killed it.

God pondered.
Half His head was jellyfish, nothing would connect.
He'd been instructed to invite the poets.
He had a rare bird this time.
Pain and blood were life
weren't they?

What's next, said Crow.
A splendid local claret, muttered God,
His words no longer everlasting,
awesome.

Crow pounced.
He bit and gnawed and sucked.
He wanted the claret complete inside him.
His deep cries abashed the academic lino
Blacker than blood.

Crow drank deep, toasted the Princess of Wails
The kingdom of darkness with indiscretions.

He just drank what he could
Ate what he could
Grabbed what he could
To keep things like this.

God guillotined further comment,
Stared stony at the gobbets.
Enough, He said, grimacing writhingly.
Earless, eyeless, great cosmic carcass.
Laureate or not, the situation cannot continue.

Crow tore off a hunk of devilled egg
Swallowed, humped, impenetrable.
Manners were lies, evasions.

The other poets staggered speechless on
Horny stricken bird legs.

God took an apple.
See this apple? said God.
I squeeze it and out comes cider.
Strictly for the birds, said Crow.
Try it, said God.

Crow gripped and clawed the glass.
Crow drank deep.

Somebody somehow was pouring his brains into a bottle
Somebody somehow was blasting his lips from his jawbones
Somebody somehow—
The spark that banged burned out his weeper.

I give up, said Crow.
Crow gave up.

All the poets met the occasion with poise.
They thanked God for his deconstruction.
They stropped their beaks.

Smiles that outflanked mouthsful of blood
Smiles that left broken gutter-pipes shattered
Smiles that left poison in a dumb place.

God, bent on restoring metric order to His Word
Sang a song totemic enough for Wednesdays
in Perth:

I am well pleased, my children,
Come and see
What wholesome entertainment
There may be.
But still you must admit
Not every day,
We fete a Laureate
In W.A.

A Canterbury Tale

(Silver Jubilee Conference of ACLLS, University of Kent, 1988)

To conference kam we pilgrims alle,
From earths imagined corners did we falle.
To live with greet disport on campus farre,
We rode by plane, by trayne, by bus, by carre.
Of studye took we care and moost heede
Noght a word spak we moore than echt was neede.
Except it be a papier for to gyve
Which is of course the means by which we lyve.
And that was all in forme and reveraunce
Both long and wyse and full of hy sentaunce
On swich as semiotic merchants thryve,
To undoe deconstructionists do stryve.
Groning with moral vertu was our speche
And gladly wolde we lerne, less gladly teche.
So amiable of port, so charming alle
No countrefete cheere did spoyle the dining halle
Where fedde we were with rosted flesh and bread
To still the sangwin nerve, the aching head.
Swich sensitive myndes, swich tendre hertes,
Were never so assembled in these partes.
(Although they say fyve honderd byshops kam
To frysk in Kentish fields in Goddes nam.)
New formes for changing cultures, wymmens plaintes,
Canon formations, languages restraintes.
All solved by Goddes grace and wynes grape,
The prykke of conscience gave us no escape.
To swich high consciousness have we been dryven
That academic sinnes are all forgyven.
Or nearly all. Theres still tyme to repent
Of energies and Englyshe pounds misspent.
So thank we all our Prioresse Lyn
Who hath for us made swich Jerusalem
In Englonds almost grene and plesaunt landes,
I ask you now to raise and clappe your handes.

I.M. William Hart-Smith

1911–1990

Whatever the reason it wasn't
your poems came first to mind,
those self-denying plants and birds
caught on revelation's edge.
No, it was a sight I can't forget
when long ago you brought the child you were
alive into a bare lecture room in Perth.

Was it Wimbledon or Hammersmith?
Somewhere in London's mean middle classes
you set us down before a timid boy
strangled in stiff collar, bowler hat,
walking reluctantly to school.
The picture stayed with me.
Only Orangemen wear bowler hats today.

The ones who set us free
fly from such tight cages into dangerous air,
how perilous only the timid know.

Easy as a pinhole piercing cardboard,
you took your eye to our strange world
to bring our sight alive.
'Just look. Keep still and let it be,'
said the poems, asking little.

You think it easy?
Try it.

PICNIC

Picnic

On a green sweep of Kings Park grass
dappled with late summer shadow
I joined a picnic with Afghani refugees,
sat sedately with the women
demure but spritely in their hijabs,
kids darting, tossing balls,
larking around, politely into food.

Meat balls, hummus and tabouli
mingled with our sizzled sausages
on paper plates. Coke and juice.
Someone had found work.
Someone had been accepted as
a lab technician. Someone's husband
still in detention three years on.
Did she get to see him?
No, couldn't get time off,
after school the kids alone
and so on.

Under a far-off tree their fathers,
uncles, brothers brooded, a still
silent circle squinting into sunlight
smoking, looking straight ahead.
Nobody seemed to be thinking of
a better world, nobody was asking
for more than a place to sit quietly
and wait. What weighs the heart must
sit it out till nightfall for release
once everyone's asleep.
And even then …

Watching all this, in and out of it,
remembering my own young wifehood
as a stranger, my first child born
in an alien tongue, the grey apartment block,
the cold, the speechless folk who passed
without a nod or smile, the men who carried
boxes piled with lurid neckties
from the Krawattenfabrik upstairs.
A condemned building.
Where would we all end up?

The tenants roused the concierge: the baby cries
all night, that pram is blocking the foyer.
Tell the foreigner.
I took it six flights up
and six flights down on sunny days.
Wasps clustered over cherry jam,
the tiny kitchen, scrubbed washboard.
Hovering useless over the baby's wheezy breath,

I rarely ventured out, avoided peak hours
in the cellar armed with shameful nappies,
took my turn with dread before
the commune's idol: a glossy water-driven
centrifuge. Its thick black snout
writhed serpentine around the tub,
soap-scummed water spewing forth
from flood-tide whine to whizz
to final cataract. Mesmerised, I bowed.

'Anyone can marry and have children,'
said my mother far away in cloud-cuckoo
land of Oz, savage with disappointment
for her accomplished daughter, all
the dead scherzos and maimed fugues.
My mother-in-law noted dust balls
gathering under the bed, the wilting
red geraniums in their box,
the cobwebbed pane.

I didn't join the turbaned band
of broad-arsed women lugging rugs
each day to the courtyard rack,
beating out the grey frustration of
their lives with rattan canes.
'She ought to be ashamed of all that dust.'
My mother-in-law's precise Hochdeutsch.
You'd think my husband's life with me
grievous enough without her fretful chorus.

Months like this as Zürich wives and
spinsters, buttoned to the neck in black,
twitched yellowing curtains, pursed their lips,
beat their fraying carpets in the yard:
tumbled boxes of neckties passing up and down
under their wordless bearers,
wasps landing, taking off.
And I, both in and out of it
learning how to live a life,
sit quiet in a cold place
waiting to touch the sun-warmed earth.

Close-up

Approaching the Great Verifier,
Lowell had one of those schizoid
close-ups with himself that come
most naturally to poets lyrically
bent. He called it 'Epilogue'.
Spurning what kept his early stuff
aloft and sailing, weighed into
plot and rhyme, demeaned his imagery
as 'threadbare', his subject matter
'heightened from life yet paralysed
by fact'. If this comes from the best
of us, what future for the rest of us?

Burn-out blues for big note orphics,
small-pond croakers brought to heel;
batteries out of juice, that's what.
Impatient with our graceless carapace
of flesh, the face that shames our
daily mirror glance, we angle for
Leviathan with a hook, lash ourselves
in poems about writing poems,
propitiate where possible, subsist on
screw-ups with our peers, our husbands,
wives, know less of men and women
than a kindergarten kid knows Dante,
fumble with the fishy and equivocal.

So 'why not say what happened?'
What makes you think we'd know?
Know thyself? A bad Socratic joke
from bearded know-alls handy with
the blanket rules. Like God,
a CEO without the common touch,
not one can help at crunch-time,
tell you how to pass for decent,
tell you why your life is skewed,

why your poems stall in scavenged diction,
stick contraptions held by string and glue.
Or why your nights are long
and black and sleepless and your
days without end are numbered.

Hokusai on the Shore

On the coast of a faraway ocean
where the sun sinks daily
a monster wave rears itself
high above a tiny figure
a young man crouched on his board.
The watchers stand fixed
on the sand and gape.

You were seventy when your wave
sprang alive. Old, ill, destitute
your money gambled away by your
grandson, your name forgotten
by the world you'd survived.
Your monster rode out
talons curved higher than heaven,
bent to envelop three boats
and their cowering oarsmen.

After all those anonymous years
beggared by petrified artefacts
your people took note, applauded,
flooded you—rewards, praise,
promises mounted. Near death
you raised life. Who among us
makes such miracles? Who keeps
a steady eye on mystery?

Quick and slow, fierce and meek,
quietly waiting came your answer:
'Until I was seventy, nothing I drew
was worthy of notice. When I'm eighty,
I hope to have made progress.'

Aceh, December 2004

Not a time for poems.
Leave fine abstractions, brass and cymbals
to the politicians, preachers furrowing
brows, parading their concern
across the archaeology of pain.
True grief is tongueless
at the site of desolation.

Better to attend the child,
dead eyes crying on the shore
for milk or comfort, frozen by the sound
of rushing water that won't leave his head.
Or catch the haunted teacher as she sits
waiting in the classroom day by day
but no one comes. Or follow the mother
scanning billboard photos:
'Looking for Asma Nabilah, aged 3½ years.'
'Have you seen Achmat Albi Jabullah, 2 years?'

Let silence speak for the fisherman
clinging to his empty net, adrift in
the poisoned air and water with the dead.
And don't forget the grandmother
wandering about, somewhere near a paddy field
she once worked … someone, maybe
someone will come home?

The Young Men

Made ghosts in all their country's wars
they come, the young men in my dreams
with shattered skulls, intestines trailing
in the sand, the mud, the stuff the TV doesn't
show unless it's Africa. Or someplace else where
colour doesn't count, democracy a word
they carted like a talisman, a passport
to the candles, bells of sainthood.

Restored to wake indoors alive, blanketed,
dreams fallen away like ash in birdsong,
sun filtering the blind slats, I'm reprimanded.
My ghosts keep talking: 'You thought you knew
it all. Tonight maybe your book and candle,
night light burning infantile, shoes tucked
neat beneath will douse your eyelids closed
with ash, shut them down for good. Our dreams were yours.

You'll sleep all right with us
and never never wake. Night lights,
books and candles lost the war against our
childhood, growing, long ago, their power
to charm away the everlasting dark a myth:
silence lasts forever. Listen, while you can,
to unseen saplings somewhere falling.'
Young men, you dear young men, I'm listening.

Makassar, 1956

We didn't fly the homeland in those days.
Lumbering P & O Orient liners slid sedately off
to post-war bliss in England; we spoke with English
vowels, revered our teachers, grieved for Hamlet
and the star-crossed lovers.
Parents, relatives and friends cried and waved,
the streamers strained, snapped, collapsed
in lollypop tangles on the wharf. Pulling away
from the tumbled web, we didn't care about
falling behind, getting ahead, dry-eyed and
guiltless went as everything was happening
somewhere else. I wouldn't have seen the signs.

Mine was someone else's colonial route,
heading for the magic islands learnt from Conrad.
I took instead a trampy old Dutch steamer,
the 'Nieuw Holland' plying the spicy archipelago
for Koninklijke Paketvaart Maatschappij, the
Royal Packet Navigation Company: wood-slatted cabin doors,
cork-chequered mats in *Badkamers*, tin dippers,
tubs for dousing, cold water tasting salty, three green
bottles in the toilet: paper was for infidels.

Decks buzzed with students going home, new
graduates from our Colombo Plan, old hands from
what was called The Indies in *tempo dulu*, stiff-backed
older lady teachers, nurses like grey Mrs Marshall from
Ballarat who'd been in prison camp and knew the ropes.
Mr Tisnadi Wiria with his wife, four children; Som and
Suparpol, the plump Thai dentists; shiny avuncular Mr Doko,
cultural superintendent from North Bali and pretty Enni
from Kadiri. And big-boned Mrs Stecklenburg with a
Victory Roll and pale apologetic daughter—the way
that woman sang! We all got into the act but respectful,

celebrating all hours and lining up for nasi goreng,
flower-cut beetroot, lobster-men, oranges and apples
for our games. The ship's lights caught us frolicking
in their benign glare.

Mornings found the sharp-nosed Aussie horse trainer,
Mr Young, rakish-angled felt hat bound for Singapore.
He used to take a daily turn around the deck, smashing
his thin Malayan wife against the rails like a rag doll.
She never made a sound. We heard he had horses and a cockatoo
on board. Later, in shock I watched her hurl a dipper
against the bathroom wall, weeping. She lived what I
had only seen on stage or read about in penny novels,
what my Nana called 'hot stuff': other peoples' lives.
Betrayal, death and homicidal rage were opera.
It must have flicked my mind to wonder how you stuck
with someone slamming your bones on what passes for
a normal morning walk, stay silent, letting it happen
over and over. Marriage, after all, meant love, an infinity
of calm water shining for miles under a new moon,
our kindly southern stars. My thoughts were virtuous,
naive, each nerve geared to heartless young imaginings,
how much better I would do it.

I ate a poisoned oyster on the Brisbane stop,
puked the north-east coast as far as the Arafura Sea.
Jovial Dr Chi's bulk filled my tiny cabin as he poked
my gut with some contempt: 'Gas, my girl, just gas!'
Offended, I lay flattened for a day, revived with Chinese
powders of a suspect green, began a letter to my mother,
tore it up: my life or what I thought was called a life
had just been launched, the world my oyster.
Never let them know and don't give up.
Dolphins and flying fish leaped and soared in the wake.
Hypnotised in hazy warmth, we dozed the afternoons
away and nightly watched Orion shift his shape.

The night before Makassar Mr Doko sang a song from Timor.
About an Australian soldier with an Indonesian girlfriend.
Hearing he's been wounded by the Japanese
she rushes off to find him, takes him to the hospital
where he dies of wounds. The tears were in our eyes
for such devotion. The girl then dresses in a soldier's
uniform, goes off to fight and gets killed too. How I
remember how we listened, how it cast us into unexpected
silence, grieving for the two young star-crossed lovers.
Mr Doko beamed with pride in his song and its effect.
Mr Eisenring looked impatient, Mr Nasiboe folded his hands:
they were getting off in the morning.

I woke to calm, the shuddering engines stopped and
through the cabin porthole saw the sea, flat, metallic,
sage-green, the ship becalmed as if in oil, still as a dream.
On deck, the soft rain fell, spindly palms fringed the
shoreline, little prahus and rowing boats swished
silently between the harbour's knolls, each marked with
a coconut palm or two just like the comic strips.
Steady rain fell on the upturned faces of the children
dotted red and yellow, blue and green waving from the wharf,
skinny arms outstretched for oranges and apples we threw.
Any minute now we'd be on land. I couldn't wait.

Boys scampered under giant banana leaves held dripping
above their heads, darting and calling. Steel-helmeted
young militia men lounged near our enchanted ship,
rifle-bayonets slung casually over one shoulder, smooth
and nerveless features gazing past us: boy-men so they seemed.
I'd never seen a gun and felt no fear: just something else
we'd read about at home. Our fathers used them in the War.
It would never happen again, we said.

After the unloading of the flour, each lumpy bag carted
down the gangway by a tribe of scrawny men, legs bowed
under the weight, scrambling fast like a moving spider's nest,
we were let out. Through Imigrasi and the stampings, permits,

questions, then released into the rain, the fragrant air
of frangipani, coconut oil, clove-scented Kretek cigarettes.
Blue smoke rose from street corner braziers charring
kambing sate sticks: our senses reeled and charged,
the crowd milling, jostling us into town while Mr Eisenring
and Mr Nasiboe disappeared for ever in a heap of luggage,
gesticulating porters and two burdened *betjaks*.

A wedding procession threaded its way along
Djalan Pintu Dua at a fine clip, embroidered silks
and gold-fringed parasols, crimson, blue and green.
First came a tall big drum, bicycle attached, the
pedals dangling from the skin, its rider thumping
forward, trombone, flutes and trumpets blaring.
My heart stood open like a door—the bride looked
very nervous sitting, eyes downcast, beside her thin
proud groom in a little cart bringing up the rear.
As it jolted past us in the warm rain, I felt a poem
starting to take shape under the reedy rhythms of the band.
It settled on my heart for nearly fifty years.

Later, looking up the Indonesia-Inggeris pocket
dictionary given me by Fong Chi Hang as I sheltered
from the driving rain in his Shanghai Sport Shop, the
phrase 'the West Monsoon' was rumoured. Can't remember how
I got to be out back eating a soup of fermented rice
and octopus with Mr Fong, his wife and lots of curious
kids or how I came to have his dictionary.
Must have needed a word for how I felt and looked up
'happy' announced 'Saja senang hati' while everybody laughed.
But I was relishing the darkened vowels, the alien softness
that spelled out my state however topsy-turvy it might be.
For once sound matched sense.

'Bahagian' was happiness and as I spoke the word,
three women passed in purdah in the street, thickly veiled
from head to toe in black like mourners. Their burning eyes
arrested me, speaking soundless of an older, fiercer order

of things. Haunted eyes that followed me in dreams—I see
them still—their black concealment hinting how
it's possible to be in one place, also somewhere else,
possible to let things happen over and over, possible
to stick in silence to pain's colours and, if it's in you,
transmit poems: burning, angry, frightened, loving, yearning
poems, rock-grooved water poems, poems of flame and
moon-flute poems, poems of the ocean and volcano's crater,
poems repeating dreams from darkness, remembering darkness.

Never in my life had I been so near to growing up
as on that day in Makassar back in 1956 watching
a wedding in the rain and the women passing.

Deckchair on the Titanic

Swag-bellied pendent canvas
stapled safe to pale archaic
scaffolding, striped symmetric
red and white
red and blue
redwhiteandblue
blue as the sea, the blood
safe between the cracks of
ice floes massing in a
gathering silence.

We are their holiday thrones:
we are British, we're American,
wir sind Deutsch. Die See ist blau.
We're whiter than ice.
We're a sure thing. Sit on us.
All around are cracks.
Something is always cracking,
Cracking up, maybe mending
pending pressures, places, times.
Mind how you sit, sir.

Everything cracks in time.
Your spine and mine. Even the book's
you're just about to browse
in peace on this the bluest
coldest sea …

External Affairs, 2nd Century AD

Imperial Trajan, Hispanic parvenu alive
And kicking rallies his Romans *in nomine patriae*
For law, order and a sound economy, ever
At pains to seem the just beneficent
Liberator—true Roman words all.

Cursing Augustan moderation in his tent
Of skin, confides *arcana imperii* to the night:
I will push our boundaries (pacing to
Crouch, scratch strategies in sand,
Ringed by his awed robotic generals),
Will overrun Africa, annex Nabataea,
Abolish the Euphrates frontier (transgression
Even blow-job Nero had to blench at),
Corral Armenia, mobilize more, more legions,
Sail down the Tigris to hit the Gulf, quell
Those dark semitic scowls of Mesopotamia.
Vassals and veterans strewn end to end will
Become Roman numerals, grinning in death.
It's *nunc aut nunquam*, freedom and martial law:
We do nothing by halves.

Throats will be artfully slit, corpses cremated
With the dignity for which we are renowned.
The smoke of our sacrifice will daily rise.
We are nothing if not *compos mentis*.
Their blood will seep back into charred
Earth amid goat turds, camel dung: under
The brooding salt hills, sandy waves of
The desert will sweep across landscapes
Of ruination, their crops blighted, their children
Starved in a cradle of slaughter.
They will be liberated.

Put the old world behind you.
My energy astounds me.
I rise from the hand of God—this
Desert air makes for apocalyptic lapses—
I glow like a comet.
I have disposed cleanly of despots,
Have disposed of those who devise evil
Against us. *Palmam qui meruit ferat*:
Let him who has won the palm wear it.

The world awaits the dawn of our devising.

The Terracotta Army at Xi'an

I **The Emperor Qinshihuang**

No epics or grandiloquent similes:
nothing in between Confucian law
Tao nihilism, one no better
than the other. Tolerance provokes
occasional civil war, or rough
reactions against formal prosody.
No swashbuckling on or off the page,
no fear of loss of face.

The timid recluse plays chess with
a Taoist priest or practises
calligraphy with a casual caller:
both sharpen their blades in silence.
Such people are biddable, landlocked,
willing subjects, ardent defenders
against foreign influence, cattle
rustlers.

At my birth drums resounded
in the drum-tower: nights of thumping
dark rhythms prefigured sinister energy
causing hot springs to overflow
their banks. To ensure I got the picture
early, my place in the scheme of things,
the kingdom's helots started construction
on my tomb the year I was enthroned:
my thirteenth birthday.

The door equipped with automatic crossbows
protected my coffin resting on a
copper base. Mercury and pearls represented
rivers, the sun and moon.
To symbolize heaven and earth
they added wild geese and ducks,
pines and cypresses.

With such fine art
I hardly needed what was left of a life.
They tell me my favourite nursemaid,
valet and concubine will be sealed alive
with me in the burial chamber's alleys,
their reward for a lifetime's devotion.

2 The Spear Bearer

Eight thousand pottery soldiers, horses,
chariots, all life-size stand ready;
Qinshihuang's imperial bodyguard poised
to march deep down into the clefts
of the Wei River Valley, down
the underworld's precipices.
Men and horses looking straight ahead
impassive for whatever fate the potter
has bequeathed their likeness to endure.

I'm fingering my armour's studs,
poking the high-fluted shoulder pads,
mutter some profane verses as I plant
my spear firmly before my feet,
striking a competent soldierly pose
to reassure my young sovereign.
He bows and offers me a niche
in his playground of immortality.

3   **The Cook**

50 beets peeled, chopped
Water
Yak milk and/or sourweed yoghurt
Black bread
Lukewarm water

Place beets in wide-mouthed jar. Cover
with water; add milk, top with bread,
cover and keep in warm place till fermented.
Three weeks to ferment. Strain and store
underground. Will keep.

Wooden benches, rough tables
scrubbed grey in our mud-brick mess,
troughs of hot coals line the walls.
Open-topped earthen ovens for the bread.

The men sit straight, top-knots tightly wound.
They inhale the onion fragrance, ever patient.
A huge kettle of brick-tea stirs over the flames
hissing and bubbling sends out a long steam cloud.

Grain spirits are stored for the generals: foot-
soldiers, archers, charioteers must stay sober,
steady hands for swords, crossbows, chariot reins.
Generals can track bird shadows over the pond,
plot tomorrow's strategies as the crane flies:
cosmic order needs no recipe,
each knows his place and fare.

My assistants chop away on a huge block:
onions, peppers, beets, lamb for the iron skewers.
The pace quickens, the voices rise.
Cabbages lie piled like split green skulls.
My soot-faced boys work hard and fast.

They dart before the bread-ovens,
splash water round the inside of the
fiery chamber, plunge their nimble hands
into the inferno, pat rounds of unleavened
dough against the oven walls. Flip, flap.
The long rods go in and out,
the pile of discs rises high and loose-leaved,
the rice steams in its vast pot heaving
with heavy puffs and spurts.
The armies wait.

Through sap-springing easterly winds,
funereal westerlies of autumn
they eat and march, march and eat.
Since I took over, sixteen kingdoms have fallen.
Food, like all human stuff, passes, is impermanent:
my master seems to value my modest fare.
He whistles softly above the hungry men,
refrains from speech.
I hold my breath.

4   The Farrier

Forty tripods and the beating boys:
scorching heat and dust mean shortened lives.
This lot know what not to expect from day one,
masks and gauntlets ranged neat on their knees,
primed for my instructions, imperial inspection.

Sunlight strikes the visors' metal bars, flashes
the length of blue-clad thighs. They're warned
to sit upright, eyes ahead: no smartass tickets
on themselves. Old hardliners are quick to sniff
conspiracies, disaffection in the workshops,
even in jest. The veteran leader's speech drones

tediously on, sclerotic elder, mouth
working away in a palsied tic, a mockery
of past eloquence. More bureaucratese.
A man of few opinions fewer words myself,
I'm safe from eloquence—practice is all.
My chief assistant pumps the bellows at my step.
We stop before each base, check measures:

breastplates for the foot soldiers,
corselets for lancers need more solid rivets
to repel sharpened spears. Flames leap higher
forced by the bellows' currents; blow harder.
It doesn't do to rattle your divine masters.
I tell the boys to keep the banter down ...

Here's a face knows little of life, the line
of his tight-shut lips as straight as a blade's edge,
forearms visible between his gauntlet's flaring cuff
and tunic sleeve, a thickness unexpected in
so young a man, tendons snaking high beneath the
lightish skin: his turn maybe tonight
to soothe the imperial choler?

I taught them tireless hammer blows,
the strike of bronze, the pincer grip,
how to curve and seal the rims,
round off the studs, perfect the shield-strap clasps.
No spear should ever penetrate these greaves.
I taught obedience as I was taught,
would lift and lay each piece before my master.
Hawk-like, he'd sweep my shining gifts aloft,
wearing his arrogance high as his pointed toque.
None had the nerve to look, so fierce the glitter
in his eye. I must have suited at the time …

Coarse and coltish, the boys roar out
to match the rhythm of the bellows' pulse.
To catch my eye, they turn and rear
like green spears of new rice plants
peeking from the flooded paddies … the master
moves methodically slow.
The visit lasts twenty minutes.

Viol strings are plucked, repeated tremolo
rising to a wild intensity in his wake.
Flutes sigh, drums shudder, hesitate for breath.
His footman follows mincing, golden parasol
raised high, respectfully above with bright
fixed eyes. That lifeless parasite!
His studied disinterest has kept boys
dangling for years.

I signal my new design, a chariot axle;
courtiers and minor functionaries have already passed,
chafing for tomorrow's falconry in gold-limned snow.
The setting sun's bright disc explodes
behind my eyelids as I make my usual deep
reverential bow, a flag obedient to the wind.
Can flocks of chattering sparrows
share the eagle's solitary path?

5   The Archer

He wanted my hands without the bow
mimed tense from the stretch.
Uneasy, I sat abstracted
in mute protest, bent the knee
against my will remembering
my father-in-law famous
as a potter. He lived exquisitely
sober. A professional aesthete
saint and sensualist but granite-
hearted. So fastidious even his
toilet was a fine ceramic urn,
daily to be filled with fresh
green cedar leaves. His wife, of course.
It didn't augur well for us.
Consummate craftsman, he taught
the virtue of the body's curve,
the contoured lines of rice fields
near our farm, jagged edge here,
polished ridge there, the waves
and furrows of wind-swept grass.

I learned my craft with game crossing
the forest haunts of bear, stag, fallow
deer, mapped the rocky routes, ravines
with stunted pines clinging to sharp
precipices, their seeds wafting in
clouds from the mountains down.
Great distances, no houses, no
shepherd's hut or cave. Severe night cold;
midsummer heat brought mist and rain.

My back is ramrod-straight
under the master's relentless measure-
taking gaze. Staring into the middle distance
I look ahead with elegant distaste
towards a point I'd rather not reach,
the target I can't miss.
Qinshihuang always saw through my subterfuge:
'Never deny your talent.
You owe it to me.'

6   The Potter

My family long gone into slavery,
my wife to early death, I wasn't too stirred up
for what was left, craved ways to take life back
so I could yield it up on my terms only.
There was a winter to be faced;
the woodpile burnt down late last spring.
I needed to go out and glean, hole up
by the mouldering hearth, look steady,
slow, no fancy moves. Remember to stay calm.
Or, as our saying goes,
'Hide your broken arms in your sleeves.'
Who am I to pit the hollow of my skull
against tyrannic arsenals, soft body parts
afloat with sewer rats, heaped skulls,
atrocities of conquest?

Trapped between potential, finished work,
I hate my feeble shuffling lurches into breath;
words dangerous, worse than fire-play.
Stick to clay, a safer recipe for silent opposition.
This ruler's outworn stratagems to put a human
stain upon a landscape, burn all books apart
from agricultural manuals, toss Confucian
analects on a pyre, pump the hearts of
simpletons with endless wars—
what price my mouse gasps?

I wasn't the only one called to serve,
more artisan than artist, random recruit
to his death-ship. Qinshihuang just happened by
as I was casting a horse's rump,
history's enemy arrested by an old man's fragment.
I assumed—wrong again—my audience would detect

the rippling tremor of irony behind my stance,
refused to bow. He laughed to show how deep his tolerance,
how insatiable his curiosity for what is commonly
passed by: the common touch indeed ...

My rage touched off a burning energy,
muscles bulging over the mould, enough to
make him start. His grin, tight as a knife-slash
stalled whatever word my slow lips formed.
At least I knew a work should never look
more finished than it is. You can't inflate
what's stodge. I started sketching men,
not to catch a likeness of what I saw.
I drew to find out what it was I saw:
something bumped against but settled for.

'I hear and I forget. I see and I remember.
I do and I understand.' As good a credo
as our sages knew: honoured, old and toothless,
banished from the present. Worth it all.
Time runs like water, drains our youth;
my moth-wing brows turn white, a phoenix
dispossessed who once had nest and children.
Will my young throw rice for my ghost?
Will they race dragon boats in my memory?

Wild ducks and geese, the jagged black rush of cranes,
the night stars, cat's mouth moon.
Remember food: pepper with honey, bitter melon soup,
lamb, turtle, sugarcane juice, the red candles,
lanterns, salt plums, lemons, vinegar,
ginger and water, rice and barley, salted eggs, beans.
Beat the drums of war and cry for the dead,
the wrongdoing. I float above the trees to the
world's roof, over the horned houses in my
dragon boat chariot of jade and ivory,
driven by cedar oars and wreathed in orchid flags,
an ice-cold vision fuelled by rage ...

The men don't like the way they look,
complain I've made their noses big,
shoulders narrow, ears a-flap.
Not how they saw themselves at all,
facing their mortality askew.
You're out to do us in, to keep your life
on track at our expense, they whine.
I don't need this task, I say. I came
because he summoned me in drink: drunk I witnessed
the wonders of the world, the unending waste of life,
imperial mendacity, the senseless sequence.
Don't forget he's your betrayer just as I am his,
but your avenger too.

The hardest is to tell the clay exactly
what I've seen, stay honest to your likeness
once the killing stops.
He wants his middens lasting, the record straight,
what was once hunted, slaughtered, eaten.
He's taking us all to a far country.
Once the great door's lowered, warrant sealed,
your tender flesh melded to the rubble of a wall,
who will care whose nose was big, whose shoulders narrow?

These days I'd rather sleep away the heat,
handy with a drunken hint of treason,
sly anarchic speechless look.
You can't get far above yourself
crumbling in the grog and camel dung,
hands crusted with a workable paste.
Stiff in the furnace stands my menagerie.
I count my bones and my luck.

Coming and Going

What they survived my children
could not bear. Or could they?
Nothing's too much or enough
as long as we live so far past
all belief.
                    Carting their deep-
grained talent for patience,
modesty, old country superstition,
they severed memory, the luxury
of talk, the stuff I stifle daily.

Just to be would do this fine
spring morning. Like a pelican or gull
wheeling the glassy river's stillness,
free from duty's churn, the world of
right and wrong I've failed to join.
Not a time for ghosts, you'd think.

But here they stand, printed stark
like huntsmen on a wall, these sudden
apparitions. Or lamps propitiatory
flaring a mind's dark niches,
testing the old life's lease,
its unsuspected corners, what every
day required in my grandmother's house:
peaceful parlour, flimsy curtains
billowing gently inward, the pianola's
yellowing keys, kitchen's radiant lino
green as emerald, squat polished ice-
chest with its magic glacier melting
each day's passing.

                And here's the
hessian-hooded iceman stooping sinister
round the corner under his block!
The chest is vaporous with hoar-frost.
He slinks out back, flywire clicks behind
to leave a riot of Morning Glory trumpets,
tendrils strangling the cyclone fence
that backed a cobbled lane; good for the
drunken sprawl I wasn't meant to see.

More alive than ever then or since
I'm summoned to the claw-foot bathtub.
The supine idol waits.
                      Eye-level with its
rounded rim I peer through steam.
My grandmother is kneeling by a tall
cylinder, stuffing its blazing door
with yellow splinters, paper, kindling
the deity to hissing, spitting life,
her day's offering to a cherished child.
Just to be was something.
I was, she was, we were.
                        It was a fine spring
morning once upon a time before I skipped,
as the Yanks say, town, leaving to lose,
to learn what I could bear.

Isfahan

The sky I've watched and walked for years
is not the heart-stopping violet-blue of Isfahan;
no golden minarets to prick or domes to contour
Waratah Avenue's electric glare.
We're dust of quite another sort here
unmesmerised by lapis shades.

But today it's warming up to summer flare;
what passes for a winter's gone.
Time to take the old wool dressing-gown
to Snow White Cleaners, tighten up
the spent elastic in my dated skirts,
change and progression in the detail.

The man behind the counter snaps me
into his virile computer. Its ticketing
paroxysm whirrs the when, the how much, and
my ancient comforter suddenly becomes Diana's
wedding dress, billows, sighs, and sinks
into professional care, a mortal thing.

From a Mercedes steps an Indian goddess of
advancing years, superb in mesmerising peacock
eyes ahead—the air is blue and green around her.
Standing erect before computer man, receives
a silken load of folded magic, violet-blue and gold
as soft and weightless as Isfahanian skies.

His dulling smile, a quarter thumb-nail moon
breaks hard above her fifty-dollar note. Neither of them
knows he's just been fingering the cloths of heaven.
What we never know is all around us
as we linger talking to the sun, the moon.

Rhyme for a Granddaughter

I took my years into my hands
And flew the wide salt seas,
To meet my frill-necked tadpole,
My heart beat with unease.

Would she know me?
Would she love me?
Old frog a-wooing went.
Rowley, powley, gammon and spinach,
My heart with worry spent

Such sleepless nights,
Such fretful days,
Why did I ever smart?
No sooner had we met again
Than straight into my heart,
Heigh ho! she leapt, my brown-eyed girl,
We'd never lived apart.

I've always chosen words with care,
The word 'love' off the list,
I feared the lie,
I would deny
The very thing I'd missed.

But missed no more
For here it is,
My wriggling brown-eyed love,
So rowley, powley, gammon and spinach,
Thanks be to what's above.

Guy Fawkes Night, 2002

Dance to your daddy,
My laughing baby,
Dance to your daddy,
Out in the dark.

His fingers are fuses,
Watch how they spark
Tall candles, bright fountains,
Hiss, fizz and bang.
Golden showers spraying
In fiery arcs hang
As turning and burning,
The darkness alight,
With barking and howling
Of startled dogs' fright.

Don't be alarmed,
My baby, my lambkin,
Don't be alarmed,
You have nothing to fear.
Nothing, I tell you,
My baby, my darling,
Just pranks that your daddies
Devise once a year.

Don't be alarmed,
My baby, my lambkin,
Don't be alarmed,
My baby, my dear.
The barrels of powder
Are locked in the cellar,
Old guy crumbles gaunt
In the leap of the flame.

The fires of rebellion
Are guttering, muttering,
Guy Fawkes now only
A faraway name.

But from ashes so grey
We rekindle this day
Of gunpowder, treason and plot.
There's more than one reason
Why gunpowder treason
Should never be forgot.

So dance while you can
To your daddy, your daddy,
Dance to your daddy,
My little lamb.

The lion and wolf will spring one day,
Ready to wreak their wicked way,
And on the fateful day they come
To detonate their home-made bomb
That day less innocent you'll be
And hear Guy's ghost in agony
Unto the heavens raise a cry:
Remember me
Remember me

Letting Go

Tell the truth of experience
they say they also
say you must let
go learn to let go
let your children
go

and they go
and you stay
letting them go
because you are obedient and
respect everyone's freedom
to go and you stay

and you want to tell the truth
because you are yours truly
its obedient servant
but you can't because
you're feeling what you're not
supposed to feel you have
let them go and go and

you can't say what you feel
because they might read
this poem and feel guilty
and some post-modern hack
will back them up
and make you feel guilty
and stop feeling which is
post-modern and what
you're meant to feel

so you don't write a poem
you line up words in prose
inside a journal trapped
like a scorpion in a locked
drawer to be opened by
your children let go
after lived life and all the time
a great wave bursting
howls and rears and

you have to let go
or you're gone you're
gone gasping you
let go
till the next wave
towers crumbles
shreds you to lace—
When you wake
your spine is twisted
like a sea-bird
inspecting the sky,
stripped by lightning.

The Duck-Herd's Night Off

Lying low on the Yangtze
under a haiku moondrift,
same old moon, same old
fraying wisps of cloud
passing over the long
flat rocks starred with
plum blossoms, gleaming
sickles of yesterday's
reed-pickers laid to
rest—all, all at the end
of my nose taking
the misty air.
                    Like my dearest,
bobbing dreamless on
the quiet current, head tucked,
so modest under the sheen
of her green wing.

Push or Knock

It's Monday, fourth of June, exactly two years
since Tiananmen Square, now happily Foundation Day
in W.A. The past lies foggily ahead, small changes
only in one's teeth and verse, a leaking roof.
We're quite grown up in our recession.

Another limbo-long weekend. I fertilise the cumquat,
wonder if the Western Waste truck's working, if
another week will pass before the garbage goes.

A morning visitor arrives: Mr Tang Zhengquiu
from Guangdong province. He's been at work
translating some Australian lyrics into Cantonese,
would like to question me about my poems.
I see them crucified by surreal consonantal clusters,
smile, and let him in.

He's thin, fine-featured and his coat is worn.
A little jumpy, takes his tea with milk,
just one small spoon of sugar.
His hand is steady, patient, offers me an essay
titled 'Sometimes Untranslatable But
In Most Cases Translatable.' For me?
How very interesting.

He asks me how I write a poem.
I bring out fourteen crippled drafts of
what's been bugging me for weeks,
a mermaid's monologue, the pages writhing
under blasts and slashes of rejection.
She's legless, going nowhere. He inspects
the murder weapons; victim's done the bunk.

I tell him that the poem's fighting decorative
scrolls, rhetoric's fancy needlework,
the sequinned tale. Does he know what mermaids are?
He says he does.
Seduced by metaphor, I wither into pedagogic prose:
'The lyric voice is struggling with the ordinary,
seams are showing, do you understand?' He does,
he says.

'In China, we say punishing the poem.'
His words give off a clang of ancient swords swung
in empty air, slicing through silk.
Are China's teeming millions all so close to poetry,
so tuned to its punitive measures? I'm sceptical.
Art's technicalities have never made our folklore.

He starts some native needlework himself,
tells of a famous Chinese poet stuck for words—
how possible? Then quotes

>   The moon shines in the sky.
>   The monk pushes the temple door

Should he use 'push' or 'knock'?

He can't decide. While worrying words around
there comes a great wise bearded seer.
Invited to resolve the matter, plumps for knock
to introduce a little ginger to the sentimental
hush. O yes, I gasp inside,
relieved to choose correctly with the blest.

How fortunate to have a visitor like that,
I say aloud. No sages pass my door in W.A.
We are our own executioners in these wide
free spaces. He smiles apologetically, then asks
if he can snap the poet at work. At work?

If you like, I say, cool as a corner neighbour:
the mermaid coils submissive to the flash.

Leaving the house, Mr Tang chats up the cumquat
blooming on the porch.
'In Guangdong province we have also
fruits like these in spring. People of Canton
make festival for them.'

From Mr Tang I've learnt that
southern China is a happy land, warmer
than the severe, meat-eating north, alive
with vegetables and bearded sages who just happen
to be passing when a poet's in a bind,
a situation in most cases
you could call translatable.

Talking Mermaid

Doing my posthumous glide, I left the amber windows
of the sea, my father's granary all Bible-black. The land
above cerulean in autumn, sun plum in a mist
so beautiful my eyelids prickled like a wounded

child outsmarting tenderness. Below, the plangent
chords, deep-sunk cathedrals tolling benedictions
to the drowned. I felt myself rising through translucent
green high on the wordless surge, once a connoisseur

of loss, stressed syllables and self-reproach,
big for my boots, myopic. Legless now
invisible to love, I'm free to circle silently.
The waterfront is murmurous with attention.

Look, dolphins! cries the waitress to her Sunday
table, Bower Lane corner café. All eyes widen,
blonde heads swivel over croissants, oranges and—
there, there, look there! two three four five

dark cleavers barrelling, soft surfers curling high
round shallow turquoise circles laced with foam
to darken, vanish, leap again in light.
No family ever moved more gently.

Close to shore they skim and roll up glistening,
morning's anthem swelling out their wake. In play
no choice, responsibility, vocation. So why
the single human head that bobs and pushes

outward, seeks to join their widening arcs?
They tease and lollop close in chorus file: his path's
presumptuous, chancey, stretching things beyond
his lineage. There is no lyric in the human stride.

See the silent watchers on the promenade leaning
outward to the shining host, the blundering head,
the flash and glide. They stand so still, suspended calm
like innocence hushed before a cortège or a ghosted

hero's speech. The young ones perch like pelicans on rocks,
crane plump over cliff and boulder, hair etched on the wind.
Their hearts are flying with the dolphins, briefly
tender, unashamed, gripped in beauty's stress,

the bobbing head irrelevant, its course imperfect.
Pure play is for the feudal few. I knew a woman in New York,
a man in France, who laughed and dolphins leapt
heaving for the open seas. Were they ever trouble!

She was a cleric's daughter, told my fortune
by the Tarot fraught with wily morose mountain men
afraid of water. Pray for a good death, always the
worry, she added kindly (still her father's child),

calling up planets lightly as you'd pick a daisy.
He was a dreadlocked *colon*, black as bronze in starlight,
slippery coaxer sprouting his burnished hydra heads
to pace each catch of breath. They lit my life,

laid nothing on me but a moment's play.
Pliant now and pruned, I trail a clownish tail,
their secret legacy, across the knives of memory.
Whoever watches creatures of the sea cavorting,

with a happy eye remember those
who made us what we might have been.
Look on this world with underwater eyes, tell
tall tales to the tongueless, take in the hiss

of water-snakes and worms sidling the skull's gape,
cruise the waterfront for song and monkey business.
Learn to breathe on land, feed tears to whales and
forecast, if you can, the grace of dolphin weather.

The Age of Aquarius

She slumps in the disabled bay
clutching a waffle-cotton gown
around a spreading paunch,
shambling breasts.
Why not say 'I'?
For that's who sits at 6 a.m.
waiting for the health club
pool to open in the rain.
A grown woman, after all,
supposed to know her whereabouts.

Today's my mother's birthday,
a 1907 Aquarian of the self-
denying kind, 'never say "I"' her motto.
She had me nailed for years. Her voice
drowns out the radio's chattering static.
Now I'm the same age she was, dying,
observing noble savagery:

a gathering knot of skinny women,
tight black butts in leotards,
regulation sneakers, Brazil-waxed calves,
gripping iPods, mobiles, water bottles.
The men stand back, silent, sullen,
balding, bored and out of it. Health stalkers,
renouncers of smoke and flame,
deniers of brimstone.
One hell of a century:
between the holocaust and the atom bomb
who are these people?

Between the deep and shallow end,
never say thank you or good morning.
Avoid eye contact.
Signals may be misinterpreted.
Slow Lane, Fast Lane, Walking Lane
Only's where I'm at.
The moving parts count laps:
twenty five's a half-hour's worth.
I sing myself a rumba to keep rhythm;
the Speedo wall clock ticks a strict 4/4
defeats my ruse while dove's feet skitter
arrow-wise across the perspex roof.

No Diving Running Eating Smiling
Share if lanes are busy.
Perhaps, perhaps, perhaps.

The waiting crowd are all, like me,
up early talking or silent,
more vivacious than galahs,
more foolish than parrots.
We stand and wait, walk up and down
in the rain talking or not, holding
in sagging muscle, spreading paunch,
talking about things that must matter.
So much seems to hang on
getting in that door.

No Return

Standing on the stump
of the self I might have been,
I crane to catch
call back those once-
huge troubling presences
receding down the road
of memory, the dearest
and the worst for whose
going I was never ready
whose end I hastened
as a child forever
waving them off, ready
to leave, always leaving
whose every footfall
kicked off avalanches
of grief in the place
I have stood upon,
am still standing,
stumped.

Interrogation

How long will you remain a child?
When the sun no longer rises.

Dawns must end.
Not when angels caper singing in the garden.

Behold the angels of old age.
See their trembling wings

Their loony lips, bewildered eyes.
They are not the heavenly host.

They left the garden long ago.
Meditate on that.

The Ivy Visitant

I cut a spray of ivy
from the yard-post near the house:
fine-cut trifoliate graded
down the curving stem
as stylised as vine leaves lacing
Bacchic revellers on temple columns
or stooping angels on a funeral urn.
So crisp and deep-to-lettuce green,
the foliage's sharpened points
pricked out late summer's
lengthening shadows.

                      Below, on
paving stones still hot from noon,
ants circled out in swarms
from nests piled dry and gritty
as tobacco dust awaiting rain.

Trailing the cutting, I went back
inside the house, turned suddenly
to feel a pest alight—a tiny
leaping thing my hand brushed off
in fright: a delicately upright
stick of fluorescent green
too rapid for the eye to cage.

Less than a half-inch long, it
jumped my shoulder down to forearm
raised its forelegs high as if
in prayer, prothorax quivering.
I shrugged it off. It clung
and prayed, its mortal desperation
severed careless from
the camouflaging leaves.

I was too large, too much in charge
making notes inside my head.
Had my daughter been around, she
wouldn't say but think as loud
as any shout, care if you must
but cut the talk. Like you
this mantis lives and dies without
the operatic blather ...

Or maybe never thought that way
at all. What's real and what's imagined?
We'll never know. What's tender is
what moves our wordless children to
forgive remembered speech, our lunatic
excesses of neglect or zeal.

That lyric enemy spewing leafage from
the gargoyle mother-mouth was us,
flesh become foliage to shelter, cast
adrift our hungry chrysalids.
Simple enough, you'd think, to know
and work it into words? It's never
what you think or what you say
but something planted speechless
in the dark, waiting out its season.

The brave viridian stick still gripped me,
steering up my arm in little jerks;
warding off its patient prayer for foot-
hold, skimmed it into darkening air
freed from the self-congratulation
of my introspection. Modest, small
it sailed into a chafing pan of stone
beneath the brazen evening sky,
the calmly circling ants.

Inside the house now silent, empty,
the way I always thought I wanted it,
telling this has failed to blur regret,
to staunch a creeping tide of radiant
green diffused translucent through
a mind (if that's the current's source)
inching snail-wise towards morning.

World Cup Spell 1998

Follow close, be swift to capture
Nestor's shield, the shining
golden prize. Strip victory from
young Diomedes, famed horse-breaker
who sports the glittering armour
of Hephaestos. Plan to conquer, Xanthos.
You Podargos, Aithon and Lampos,
hurl back the Greeks, hold off
the desperate lady Hera raising hell
on Mount Olympus, slandering
philandering Zeus ...

                    So spoke Hector,
shook the Trojans into Iliad mayhem.
                So do I, and
forty-six percent of Buddhist monks
in Thailand barrack for the
diving dragon-seed tonight,
flowing-haired Brazilians, warlocked
warriors of the Cup, winged
names Apollo's lyre would once
have leapt to praise:

Mighty keeper Taffarel, icon untranslatable,
matchless Cafu, full-back glorious,
Roberto Carlos, scourge of all midfield
defences, hard man Dunga, heraldic captain,
airborne Junior Baiano, young Rivaldo,
virtuous shooter, right-wing César Sampaio
of the Yokohama Flugels, hairless
Ronaldo, Leonardo, *anarchistos*,
fabled strikers, Botafogo's keen Bebeto,
flare to swoop on upstart *colons*.

Hurl back Lizarazu, Barthez. Ward off
Karembeu, Thuram, Djorkaeff.
Break predator Zinedine
Zidane, Algeria's dark magician,
monkish twister licked to glide
by serpent tongues. Freewheeling names
that strut and weave, circling earth
like echoing gongs pulsating in space—

Wing this incantation to my heroes
as I sit, couch potato frustrate
in the hollow anglo-saxon silence,
repulsing tides of mediababble
jargon yeah and yeah again,
cued in reverberant by salvationary
bands—summer frogs, cicadas and
the dry archaic magpie fangling away
upstream before the rain.

Starting Over in Autumn

Halfway wise when young,
who could forsee their stubborn mysteries,
their presumptions of innocence?

They intended to disappoint nobody.
Who could have warned them?
Who would have listened?

Can they imagine today what nobody knows,
the span of a human breath
coming and going?

He thinks she can.
She hopes he might.

And why, you ask, does the poet
(jotting under the broken angel's wing
at the bottom of the garden) sound off
such lamentatory alarms?

Observe the verdant celebrant in his hot suit.
He's not reading the sorrows of Job
unsuited to such modern occasions.
Is there anything you would like me to say?
He has a gold biro rolled behind his ear
for the record, smiles on the dotted line:
hello my friends
we are gathered ...

What lasts is what they started with,
the faltering heart and something else.
Nothing won or absolutely lost,
still here imagining a place
where people work and pray and sleep,
the tender rituals of surrender.

Time has changed sides, no longer on theirs.
She almost knows.
He doesn't want to know and doesn't
know he doesn't.

The poet doesn't like those lines.
Forget the poet at the garden's end,
what he knows and can't forget.
He's called today a day like any other.

The earth's still green,
birds hop in the yard in hopeful rain,
the young still wait, gravid with yearning.

Pray for them, their children, and those birds.
Let them attend the grace of candour or whatever
waits behind the soul's clear windows.

Adios, Buenos Aires

Northbound talking to God
gabby as ever delivering
the usual earful of next-
world projects all in the
fullness of time and I'm stuck
in turbulence at a perishable
altitude querying truth
whether the preposition belongs
at beginning or end and why
in His name the plane is
shuddering, dropping, remembering
father, tap-dancer, fornicator,
dauber of socialist slogans
in of all places Argentina
embattled by rumour that mother
was cleaning house for the Perons
and about to publish a scurrilous
memoir trouble enough you'd think
without me hope of the side
taking off in a stolen plane
cajoling the Boss in fractured
Portuguese getting above myself.
As usual.

Cogito

Redundant, middle-aged, for
makeshift shafts of time
adrift in shady fantasies,
he's found and lost the plot.
So what, he thinks, dead-pan
as movie heroes might. To fill
the day, he wanders scarce-
equipped to meet new-fangled
life: bank robbers, beggars,
muggers, porn-shop entrances
and exits.   He is thinking,
therefore he exists among
quotidian signs and wonders,
never suffers circumscribed
unravellings that writers put
you through but minor dips
into imagination's tide:
what might be taking place
in other heads, believing
he's opaque, transparent
all at once, like anyone
with anything to hide.

How do conductors know
exactly who has paid the fare?
Who has got on, got off,
the when and where?
Whenever ticketless he tries
to weather what's afoot,
conceal the sleight, sit still
but always finds the patient
watcher near his shoulder
trained to spot the guilty
twitch, the lowered head
(*he'd* know for sure his wife'd
been cheating on him seconds
after coming home).

He knows for sure
he'll never know what everybody
seems to know. Or do they?
Buttoning down the doubting surge
he wanders double-thinking
with himself to take a lift
and ponders why the 14th floor
is actually the 13th.
Never worked it out. If danger
lurked in 13 wouldn't 13th floor
be dangerous no matter what
its name? Would God be bothered
by a number switch? They
(who are 'They' anyway?) must
consider deity a humbug if
they thought He wouldn't twig.

What kind of world is this
that hands us questions,
answers of this sort? What
are we like, he thinks, if
this is how we catch ourselves
in thought, a spectacle
avoiding making of ourselves
a spectacle?
      More like a spectre,
guessing when and how we might
meet death, escape the train
conductor's gimlet stare, or,
peering at libidinous magazines
with awe, too coy to pick one
up, ducking the fat man at the
till's bored gaze, still
pondering that 13th floor.

Genesis

Shuffling phrases, images like card stacks,
what's it going to be?
Not one fixed notion for a kick-start.
Rather something stumbled on at night
(the dark is best for stumbling),
chancing it blind, spoiling for a fall.

Will it be one more bulletin from the zone
of dread? Another bleat of unbelonging?
Or some grim soot-faced riff on the long-dead,
the incantatory singsong of nostalgia—
serial murders, violated wombs, decay,
the foot-in-mouth neuralgia of our days?

You thought you knew how life began, ran
smooth across that golden horse-shoe bridge?
The ground can cave in anywhere, undreamt-of
mystifying shifts and gaps, like waking up
one day without your face to say
I cannot recognise this life as mine.

Whose is it then? Just sitcom stuff,
a laugh a minute? But only if you're slanted so.
Try this one for a fix of the uneasy kind:
the Irishman who told me, poker-faced, how
walking on Westminster Bridge the other day
ran smack into Pat Hegarty.
'So Hegarty,' says I, 'how are you?'
'Pretty well,' says he, 'thanks, Donnelly.'
'But Donnelly,' says I, 'that's not my name.'
'Faith, neither Hegarty is mine,' says he.
So then we looked hard at each other
and sure it turned out to be nayther of us.

How's that for seismic shift? It's what
you can't trim down to manageable that
seeds the poem, keeps the poet sparked
awake to what could be, to what might
fan him into flight. Better not to know
but stumble unawares on randomness,
like walking mapless in an unknown town,
get recklessly resiliently lost without
your face or life you thought you knew.
The poem will either find
or find you out.

Poetry Promenaded

They hear you're reading
on a Sunday in a garden
somewhere in the city of
light and the sad wry smiles
adjust the angle of
their eyebrows telling you
how sorry they are
that something else is on
and you start wishing that
it was the same for you,
prey, as always, to premonitions
of the darker kind.

But it's not a rational world
and because you are a poet
you start imagining a garden
meaning grass and trees and
birds and gentle light and
lovers lounging, children rapt,
drowsy grandmothers, a hermit
or two, an emperor awake to
prophetic nightingales and
clusters of attentive courtiers
hanging on your every word,
the last sounds of this wing-
tip language spoken personally.

But a flat-vowelled crow takes you
briskly aside, snaps your fantasy
adrift, tail feathers bristling:
'Have you forgotten that it's
free which means that five or
six will amble past and gawp,
take in a word or two, regret
the spunkless void, move on?
Two men and a dog if you're in

luck, no golden boughs for you,
you drongo (his slang as dated
as his lingo). If you were a wise
bird which you aren't, you'd stick
to water, shade, and worm-delivering
lawn and cut the hokum. Stop imagining.

The emperor's been sleeping it off
for centuries, the grandmothers are
peddling dope, the hermits raiding
the casinos, the children passing
cool through their academies, the
courtiers shredding loot in paper
bags so give up on the crap. You're
more defunct than Patagonian Tooth-Fish.
Admit it's over for you guys—or,
if you must go through with token
stunts, stick in a line or two
the management will take for
compliment regardless that they've
got you by the short and curlies.'

'Get lost!' you say, poking
the mocker with an angry stick
the harder since he's known
for telling truths that no one
wants to hear. You steel yourself
to read your poems
just one more time
in a garden
somewhere in the bruised-
heart city of chrome
and steel and concrete
which is exactly where
you are
you are
you are

NEW AND UNCOLLECTED POEMS

Bedfellows

On finding Judith Wright and John Manifold in Modern British Poetry, New and Enlarged Edition, *in Florida 1984*

What are they doing there?
What are they doing?
Sad and bitter celebrators of
their country's truth?

We may no longer be confusable with Austria
Asturias or Austrât (those films,
that Cup, the ever-squawking thornbird)
yet more than water separates
an A from B.

In the tidy wastes of haveagoodwhatever
and yallcomeback, the gorge also
rises to find Manifold bound:
  Tomorrow like another day
  I draw the dole and rust away
      together with
  Bored, uninformed, knowing the ghostly silt
  Dispersed, yet tending to this cross of ground.

Nor does it wow me finding
  Look the whole world burns
  The ancient kingdom of the fire returns
      sit down as kin to
  Why need I fear the bursting bomb
  Or whatsoever death shall come
      in the same old
      double binding.

More than diction parts us here.
To bear the world or not to bear.
But when our time has come and gone
in the shrill kingdom of the dumb,
shall we still shrink against a throne?

Madam C*

Who does she remind me of,
this beady bourgeois Brünhilde
leering from the jacket of my Pushkin?

That sneaky tight-lipped squint,
darting black pinhole eyes,
fussy bonnet ribboned like a cake.

A hint of double chin reared plump
above the tight lace collar, high-
waisted turquoise satin robe
crossed by one imperious finger.

A modern harridan in her dressing gown.
The sidling whippet's sceptical.
What mood have we today, ma'am?

She's not the Queen of Spades
this sinister old bird in charge,
eyes heartless as a crow assessing worms.

Half-smiling, permanent in power she
rules the roost. I know you now,
you Prussian prig. Scarce one free peasant

left in Russia at your death. Like Madam C,
my old sadistic piano teacher, Magyar migrant
claiming kinship with Franz Liszt via Bela B.

She took her landing in Australia hard,
remained to die among the rusted cans,
the sharpening axes of a tone-deaf peasantry
and lolling lizards whistling in the spinifex.

* Portrait of Catherine II walking in Tsarskoie-Selo in 1794 by Vladimir Borovikovsky, Tretyakov Gallery, Moscow.

Domestic Architecture

The Wife

A rotary hoist in the front garden
and he's an architect. She's glad
he's rarely home, has even learnt to pardon
a plaster Atlas staggering sad

under a crushing ball among the ferns.
She founders over broken toys,
a rusted cycle in the grass, and yearns
for order. They are childless. It annoys

the neighbours when she nightly sings
    'O neighbours, neighbours, I am growing old.
    My husband built a house and gave me rings.
    The house is dark, my child within grows cold …'

The Architect

She always wanted it, that line.
Against my will I put it in
to please her. Things were fine
till Mum gave us that statue. Always thin,

I couldn't bear the load. I stayed out late,
came home to find her tripping and falling
in grass I couldn't tend. My mate
was heard crying and angrily calling

about some child and a house. We had
no kids. I really don't know why
she made a fuss and it's too bad
to think the neighbours heard the cry …

The Neighbours

We don't know why
our neighbours cry ...

A Small Variant on Intelligence

Somewhere I read that
deeply corrugated brows denote
a limited intelligence.

My brow is furrowed deep.
I thought it was myopic strain in childhood,
memory's cold puzzles, great ideas.

I couldn't see to read.
I couldn't see to see.

But yesterday the ferry drew its length
clean from the wharf's rim out into
a sun-filled harbour and moving slowly out
a smile began to spread my mouth
parting smoothest water furrowed fine as silken thread.

Pure happiness, I thought.

And as I thought the word,
the sunny harbour drenched in light and water
shrank to what the writer
had in mind.

Primal Dreamcake

What a night and they keep saying
nothing happens in Tasmania!

Just stopped watching this uplifting
bit of Whitman, oceanic swell
gratitude for life even for the humblest
creature down to Walt's noiseless patient

spider, containing multitudes
at one with creation acknowledging the perfect
fitness and equanimity of—God, there's a
spider on the toilet roll, patient,
hasn't moved for twenty seconds.

Trembling in the doorway bladder
bursting but I can't go in I can't
move anywhere I have to keep my eye
on him.

He might shimmy under the seat
lower himself into the laundry basket
fold his hairyness in the tissues
lurk among the pegs
all legs or spin himself
king-size in the twin-tub.

Love of life's draining out o stevedores
brakemen and blacksmiths where are you now?

I'm not enamoured of men, Walt, can't eat
and sleep with them week in week out one would be
particularly welcome now I can't sleep
with the spider in the bathroom.

Let it put its ductile anchor some place else
mark its little isolated promontory
stalking someone else's loo a conservationist
a greenie must be oodles in Tasmania why
pick me meanwhile the spider's nipped inside
the cardboard roll one hairy leg waves out
I tell him in a strangled voice stay there
you bastard wait till I get back and
run the lights are on next door
I knock a woman says she's got no spray
and no she won't come out and no she
can't do anything her door stays shut
the slut I've given up on sisterhood.

Two legs waving now, a friend swims into mind
she lives close by I phone she'll come
a pal at nearly midnight reads her Whitman
knows the Bible backwards comes from Queensland.

She arrives bearing like the grail a green
cloth enfolds the roll with reverence bears out
the nightmare lets it loose at the street
corner purring Lovely baby and she wanted to
kill you did she
To sleep perchance to browse Fay Weldon's latest
blast against wet English flute jobs piping
Pergolesi news about Jelallabad polluted rivers
and dreaming soon a woman with pale eyes pale
hair those marvellous British bones who has
to be Venetia or Antonia competitive about
her children snug in Ladybirds who play
the flute the harp the violin
and probably the dulcimer who doesn't want
to hear about my children whose baby photos
I can't find whose beauty I can never
forget I'm trying to make a school lunch
for my daughter but there's no food she
doesn't want to eat and milk is spilling

out from strange places puddles of white
glop keep spreading   spreading—
the woman's husband is a pompous bore
prancing on a shoreline in new Guccis
recorder at the ready braying Must you
bring out all those photographs is all this
necessary can't you get rid of her and we
know all there is to know about music come
here Portia and we'll show her who can play
and sing and do such miracles her children
daily do we know much better don't we.

They all sit on a golden cloud and leave.
He'd have to be a Hubert Osmond Cecil
there's no Bill or Jim to back me waking
weak—
would Whitman stay alone in a bathroom
with a spider? Never trust a poet
watch their actions not their speech
before you go to bed observe the
Ayatollah or anyone who's got a
finger on creation's pulse.

Banksia Menziesii

Dragon-pods swell,
feathered birth,
armoured transience.

Casting the Die

Only Joseph Brodsky would be daft enough,
Only *The Times Lit. Supp.* could print this stuff,
(or the *New York Review of Books*, a friend of Auden
after all, reputedly dissident):

'The poet, the loved one and the Muse' proclaims the heaven-sent
gospel: only men write poetry of love, woman can't be other
than love object, muse, or, if she's suitably adroit, a mother.
She may write poetry herself, but by a whisker.
She doesn't match the masculine paradigm, the apparatus of desire
can only frisk her,
never penetrate the depth. Nor can she turn a verse to potent thrust
and melt of sexual conquest, her ineffectual trust
in smaller things debars her from the Brodsky canon.
She's jealous, callous, hopeless. This is 1990. More anon:

O my hornbill husband, you have a bad smell,
and when Kaaeko comes and smells you
he will take you to Panirai and your spirit
will enter a pig. So runs a Buin wife's lament
for her spouse, lost from view.

Expressing love takes unfamiliar tracks, the ironing board,
the kitchen sink, the loo:

What a hot glide up, then down, his shirts
I ironed out my father's back, cramped
and worried with work.

Or

Sometimes shaping bread or scraping
spuds for supper, I have stood in the kitchen,
transfixed by what I'd call love
if love were a whiff, a wanting for no
particular lover,
no child, or baby or creature.

The object of my desire may be arachnid,
sprawled behind the toilet door, splayed on a leaf.

I have left you four flies.
Three are in the freezer near the beef,
the other one is wrapped in Christmas paper
tied, I think, with reefer knot
in pink.

There's love, as an arachnophobe can vouch,
more diverse than mere lusting on the couch.

So what does Brodsky think male poets want?
The vacant leaves his mind's imprint bear out.
Male poets seek, he gargles, *visually aleatoric blondes*
over the excessive precision of brunettes.

So that's it. Aleatoric pets.
Aghast, I look it up.
Unpredictable, it says, dependent on
the dice's throw, the dyer's cast,
from Latin 'aleator' meaning gamble.

That cuts me out who nightly amble
scarps of lateral thought with markers of
bi-lateral agreements.

Does this mean non-Caucasians needn't apply
to be commemorated in those deathless odes and sonnets?
If hairs be wires, black wires grow on their heads,
and in their hearts, laid neatly end-to-end beneath their
bonnets
if Brodsky be believed.

Dark or fair, if they have wits, do know that love is short,
forgetting long.
That never blocked a poet from a song,
whether in greed and haste they do infect and curse
each other like Robert Graves and Laura, Sylvia and Ted.
Or worse, display their verse for all to read with dread.
Although we're told that literature's not life,
there are more ways to kill than with a knife.

Queen of ingratitude, to my dying day,
You shall be punished with a deathless crown
For your dark head, resist it how you may.

So, if you live dark ladies, remembered not to be,
Die blonde, or else your image dies with thee.

The Witnesses

This morning, stirred beneath the agitation of the rain
came three white-collar magpies to my lawn.
Jehovah's Witness-like they knocked
they knocked upon my window pane,
stood black demanding entrance. I held my ground
but they were smart and oh-so-keen,
so upright, firm they pushed their song at me,
surprised my shrinking soul.

'Spare my breath,' I said, 'you've fangled
on my lawn all night. Enough's enough.
What more have you to tell?'
'O foolish pale and puny earthling,
save your wit—our glamorous warbling
has unlocked the last old secrets of the soul.
Go warm your winters fast against the
rising dark, the setting sun,
the climbing moon, the mourning grasses
and the chill of the dusk.'

Pages

After Cavafy

Sitting late into the night,
cluttered table, old books,
clumsy commentaries on long-
forgotten texts, a lost world in my head.
My life as full of names
as an abandoned cemetery or
phone book in a foreign city,
the city of my ancestors.

See where it stands, so glossy,
vibrant, new, a lure for export only.

I stare at a half-finished loose iambic
mix, formal twinned with the vernacular,
pushing up from some lost seedbed
where the roots began: parents who loved
me, suffered big words from an unfledged beak,
friends dead, lost or mad, private mirage of
solace looming, vanishing.

Were summer evenings ever so alive with birds?
So tranquil? Was the sky that blue?
Who really lived there?

The barbarians have taken my city,
its citizens barnacled to ancient rites.

The homeland trap: huge silences
over the dark bluestone streets once
sites of transgression, the wrong company.
Done in by dangerous allure, I flew the coop,
letting fly to learn by leaving
what I knew, growing old imagining.

A woman with a notebook in her hand
turning pages like wings.

My Dachshund Schnitzel

I will consider my Dachshund Schnitzel
For she is the most beautiful of all creatures
Created by the living God whom she
In her own way worships,
Insinuating her long slow body
With lumbering lurches
Between the chairs and table as,
Urged on by her ambitious owner,
She patters towards the shimmying rat
Up the curtain rim. And misses.
She hears the words of the Lord through
Long delicate ears of marvellous softness
For she is most beautiful of all creatures.
Questing for crumbs and bones her
Shining black nose woozles across the carpet
While the Lord watches over her roly-poly torso
So gravely elongated, and her docile soul
For which I give thanks and pray
That her end will be calm and painless.

Reasons for Play

Spruce from their analyses
those soulful characters,
spectacles driven backwards
across furrowed balding fronts,
intoned: 'The trouble with you,
you never learnt to play.'

Said in such tones that
what could she feel but
drab and heavy which
is today's word but
nonetheless friendly.
And she laughed about the
rough end of whatever
it was she'd clutched.

'Yes, you are so right'
she said, furious with
concentration and an old
handicap: 'Morally, I have to
stay out if it. My absolutes
have proved dodgy but yes,
I've never learnt to play.'

And born to the Freudian
persuasion, she continued,
'While I was being the eldest son
you never were, you were earnestly
at play with Elizabeth and Ellen,
Elaine, Evelyn and Etcetera'
which were the popular
names of the period and
not to be lightly spoken.

Eldest girls don't play early or
lightly. Clamped by mysterious
authority requiring lineaments
of gratified desire, they look
obsessed and condescending,
but are negatively capable.

Eldest girls believed, born to
the Freudian habit, that all
could be explained, with a belief
that even Hitler, Stalin, and
war's fires could not destroy, that
there was always reason
behind frightfulness.
They couldn't leave a burning house
without trying to help the arsonist.
Who knew how to play.

They travelled blind, naïve to
universe's rim like their great
grandmothers who'd fled the old
world's burning houses, voices
turned to ironies of apprehension.

Like them, they learnt the new
land's language late, became
its wary fire wardens, learnt
how to warn without accented stammer,
learnt how to leave a burning house
alive, divest themselves of glut
and test whatever solo flight
could bear once they took wing.

Charon

Twelve noon Monday, 38 degrees and rising.
The phone's rung twice
and someone else has fallen off
the twig while military files of micro-
ants move in on ancient crumbs.
Who said we'd live forever.

And yet (the strand of memory unscrolls)
and yet I hear as clear as yesterday
the lines I spoke as Charon
in our Latin class's play, circa 1942:
'Manum mihi da, puerum,
pulsum sentiam.
Obolum mihi da.
Morituram te salute.'

Never let them tell you Latin's dead,
snorted Beatrice Short, BA Hons.
ramming a rolled-up map of
Imperium Romanum into poor dyslexic
Margot Dumbrell's rib cage.
The language of oppression
sticks forever.

Our fathers were at war.
We'd read about the dead-eyed ferryman
a grubby bugger meanly clad
in our abridged *Aeneid*
wheedling proof of death,
a silver obolus, some antique coin
placed on the tongue before burial.

My mother, innocent of pagan rites
preferred a prettier role for me,
something garlanded and girlish,
Persephone at least. But I was dark
and death-drawn early, chose to rub
against the girly grain. We'd grown up
graven with a sharp dynastic proverb:
'Have it but pay for it.'

Charon's stern allure sat too familiar
on my stubborn head: 'You want to die?'
Well, pay for it. Behind the mask
I spoke with a flourish, nothing forgotten,
nothing grasped between this world
and the next.

The distant shore blurs, lost in fog.
There's water between us, I'm here
on the bank getting used to so many
leaving, ceasing ceasing to be
beginning again, rising from where
the roots began
to face

Little Fly

After John Bunyan

My Mužka ('little fly' in Czech)
Goes softly but she goeth sure.
She stumbles not as larger creatures do,
Her journey's shorter so she may endure
More puissant than do those who further go.

Right at my feet she canny curls,
She makes no noise but delicately paws
The bony beast appointed for her meal,
Feeds quiet, a marvel of containment.

Her modest inch of soul shines clear
From liquid eyes, the tail divine wags
Neither fast nor slow but sure.
Most certain is it that for those who journey so,
The victor's garland they will fast procure.

In Rehab

Dr Kiberu comes at dusk
pierced with the passion of dense knowledge,
a cool Nigerian cat in Black,
geriatric oncologist supremo.
His winking buckle guides my eye. I've been so lucky.

Propped on my air mattress like the Pope
taking stock from a high window, a grand
river vista shrouded in mist, dotted with
little lights, my head full of Wordsworth and
Westminster—O school, O poetry, O history—

The river glideth at his own sweet will:
Dear God! the very houses seem asleep;
And all that mighty heart is lying still!
Not everyone has been privy to such visionary
company: was ever such a time before or since?

After long silence my broken world sits sweet
with memory, its beauty dries my tongue.
He said it's not the best news, could be worse.
There are two kinds: aggressive and less aggressive.
Are you religious?

I said I could be but not so you'd notice.
Religion's not my business, said the doctor.
Comfort, maybe. I wish I'd better news for you.
Being well brought up I thanked him warmly.
My mother would have been so proud.

At least some things we shared—our shortened
breath for one. And Dad would have produced his
corny oft-repeated joke about all being quiet

on the Western Front. I didn't get it in the old days
but couldn't face his halting repetitions, feigned
to know the gist in our formal family way: there
would be all those years ahead to understand.

Boat Song

Speed, bonnie boat, like a bird on the wing,
'Onward', the seekers cry;
Speed, you will not, but sink like a stone
Down on the seabed lie.

'We once had a country', the desperate cry
'Now we're officially dead'.
The Ministers grin, 'You cannot come in.
You'd consume all our daily bread'.

The debris of massacres, blitzkriegs and bombings,
Putsches and pogroms, war's goings and comings.
Tyres are for burning and cobbles for throwing.
Army surplus for wearing and weeds fit for mowing.

Lie in military tents with fear gripping breath,
Forget that you're living, expecting a death.
Remote ideologies send bonnie boats
Like broken-winged birds to our merciful votes.

And we turned them away, yes we turned them away
As we went out to play
In our dead-hearted country, the bounteous place
Where neighbourly love puts a smile on each face.

As we golf and we gamble, eat, make love, and die,
Raise shrines to our roadkill, release a brief sigh—
Only heaven knows why—and for hours upon hours
We bring photos and candles and
Mountains of flowers upon flowers upon
Flowers upon flowers.

Droughtbreaker

No sooner resolved never
to write another line
the habit of resolution
being so strong,
the air turned suddenly
sweet outside her window—
the longed-for stirring slow-start
hesitant splutter, first rain's
rustling pitter over pear tree
eucalypt and star-studded stephanotis,
gripping her round the heart
deep into wakening dark where
the canny chortle of enchanted
magpies let her gently go

In Memoriam, JB

You're leaving us
the things you found (we found) so hard
to speak about—the books, the films,
the high beam on your car, political shenanigans
that split us wide apart, the things we never
could agree upon, you on the right,
me on the left.

I well recall the night before the Iraq invasion
shouting at you over quaking scallopini at Valdarno's
tears streaming down my face, specs all misted over—
can't you see?
can't you see?
why won't you see?

And you, polite, calm, infuriatingly right,
the tactful English gentleman confronting
the unruly desperate Australian virago.
What's the matter with the woman?

True grief is tongueless (as I once said
in an early poem about lost love).
I still believe it.
We never learn, dear John.
We've grown up like a pack of frightened kids
standing in the corners of the world,
graduates of the school of inhibition, cum laude,
wary of weapons of mass destruction,
the biggest of which is death.

We're learning …

We feared that love was not enough.
You doubted your own goodness.
We never did. But now are left
to linger guilty in your debt.

We only ever yield to love
when someone's dead or gone.

www.ingramcontent.com/pod-product-compliance
Lightning Source LLC
Chambersburg PA
CBHW030516230426
43665CB00010B/643